Helen Mitcheson is a solicitor with extensive experience at the intersection of law and marine mammal science. Before qualifying as a solicitor, she worked as a marine mammal scientist and consultant in the UK, Canada and the United States. She holds an MRes in Marine Mammal Science from the University of St Andrews – one of the first graduates from this internationally respected programme – and an LLM in Environmental Law from Newcastle University. Her legal and scientific expertise underpins her work, which involves advising developers, consultants, statutory bodies and NGOs on the legal frameworks affecting marine mammals in UK waters.

A recognised leader in the field, she has been listed on the ENDS Power List of 100 environmental professionals making the greatest impact in 2022, 2024 and 2025. She regularly lectures on marine mammal law, including at the University of St Andrews, and has presented on this topic at major conferences such as the United Nations Ocean Conference, the Society for Marine Mammalogy, the European Cetacean Society, the European Environmental Law Forum and the UK Environmental Law Association.

A Practical Guide to Marine Mammal Law in the UK

A Practical Guide to Marine Mammal Law in the UK

Helen Mitcheson,

Solicitor, BSc (Hons), MRes, LLM

Law Brief Publishing

Published 2025 by Law Brief Publishing, an imprint of Law Brief Publishing Ltd
30 The Parks
Minehead
Somerset
TA24 8BT

www.lawbriefpublishing.com

Paperback: 978-1-918241-02-0

Hardback: 978-1-918241-04-4

PREFACE

This is the book I wish I had throughout my career.

When I first began working in marine mammal science and later qualified as a solicitor, I found myself navigating a complex and often fragmented legal landscape governing marine mammals in the UK. There was no single reference point – no clear guide that brought together the multiple legal frameworks and interpretations of how these laws apply in practice in the context of marine mammals. Over time, I realised that this absence wasn't just academic inconvenience; it had practical consequences for regulators, developers, consultants, scientists, conservationists and legal professionals alike.

Marine mammals – including cetaceans (whales, dolphins and porpoises) and pinnipeds (seals and walrus) – face growing pressures in UK waters from human activity: disturbance, bycatch, habitat loss, underwater noise, changing ecosystems and climate change. The laws intended to protect them are spread across different regimes – wildlife protection statutes, fisheries regulations, environmental assessment rules and marine licensing procedures – and their implementation can be inconsistent, reactive or unclear. While there are excellent resources on environmental and wildlife law more broadly, none address marine mammals with the dedicated attention their legal status and ecological importance demand.

This book aims to fill that gap. It brings together in one volume the legal frameworks relevant to marine mammals in the UK and sets them out in a way that is structured, accessible and useful. It explains how the law applies in practice, identifies challenges in interpretation and enforcement, and reflects on areas where reform is being discussed.

It is written for practitioners: for solicitors, barristers, in-house counsel, policy advisors, environmental consultants, academics, researchers and others who work at the intersection of law and the marine environment. My intention is not to advocate, but to inform – to provide a clear, grounded and reliable reference on the relevant law that will help others navigate this area with greater confidence and clarity.

In writing it, I have drawn on my experience as both a marine scientist and a practicing solicitor, advising clients from statutory bodies to offshore developers to NGOs. I've also benefitted from opportunities to teach, present and collaborate across disciplines, all of which have shaped my understanding of how marine mammal law operates – and how it could evolve.

It is my hope that this book will not only serve as a guide to what the law currently says but also prompt careful reflection on how these laws might be reformed in the future.

The law stated in this book is believed to be up-to-date and correct as of 20 September 2025.

Helen Mitcheson
September 2025

ACKNOWLEDGEMENTS

I wish to express my heartfelt gratitude to Nina Pindham and Richard Broadbent, whose expertise in environmental law has been both inspiring and invaluable throughout my career and in the development of this book. Their unwavering support, from encouraging me to transform my aspiration of writing this book into a tangible achievement, to providing meticulous reviews of my work, has been instrumental. I am deeply appreciative of the insightful discussions we've shared, which have significantly enriched the exploration of key topics within these pages.

CONTENTS

INTRODUCTION

The territorial[1] and offshore[2] waters of the United Kingdom hosts over twenty known species of marine mammals, including cetaceans (whales, dolphins and porpoises) and pinnipeds (seals and walrus[3]). Among the most encountered cetaceans are the harbour porpoise (*Phocoena Phocoena)*, bottlenose dolphin (*Tursiops truncatus)*, common dolphin (*Delphinus delphis)*, white-beaked dolphin (*Lagenorhynchus albirostris)*, Risso's dolphin (*Grampus griseus)*, orca (*Orcinus orca)* and minke whale (*Balaenoptera acutorostrata)*. Larger migratory species such as humpback whales (*Megaptera novaeangliae*), fin whales (*Balaenoptera physalus)*, sperm whales (*Physeter macrocephalus)* and pilot whales (*Globicephala spp)* are increasingly recorded in UK waters also. These species vary in size, behaviour and sensitivity to threats, which include bycatch and entanglement, underwater noise, recreational pressures, vessel strikes, pollution, prey depletion, habitat degradation and the escalating impacts of climate change.

1 The territorial sea of the UK extends up to 12 nautical miles (nm) from the baseline, as defined in section 1 of the Territorial Sea Act 1987. The baseline is typically the low water mark around the coast, and the UK baseline is delineated in the Territorial Waters Order in Council 1964 (as amended). Nautical miles are used to measure the distance travelled through water. A nautical mile is slightly longer than a mile on land, equalling 1,852 metres. The nautical mile is based on the Earth's longitude and latitude coordinates, with one nm equalling one minute of latitude.

2 For the purposes of this book, offshore waters refer to those within the Exclusive Economic Zone (EEZ). The EEZ extends from the outer limit of the territorial sea to 200 nautical miles from the baseline or to the median line with another coastal state's EEZ. The UK EEZ is outlined in the Exclusive Economic Zone Order 2013 (SI 3163/2013).

3 Sea lions are also pinnipeds, but since they are not found in the wild in the UK, they are not discussed in this book.

Some populations are year-round residents, such as coastal groups of bottlenose dolphins and harbour porpoise, while others are transient or seasonal visitors. Additionally, recent years have seen increasing reports of vagrant species, including Arctic species like the beluga whale (*Delphinapterus leucas*) – notably spotted in the River Thames in 2018 and in Shetland in 2024. Deep-diving beaked whale species have also been identified, sadly as a result of stranding along the UK's coastline.

The UK is also home to two resident pinniped species: the grey seal (*Halichoerus grypus*) and the harbour (or common) seal (*Phoca vitulina*). Occasional sightings of vagrant pinnipeds – such as walruses (*Odobenus rosmarus*) and ringed seals (*Pusa hispida*) – have also been recently recorded.

Pinnipeds are both terrestrial and marine in behaviour, using coastal haul-out sites for critical life stages such as resting, breeding and moulting. These haul-out sites vary in accessibility and environmental exposure, ranging from open beaches to secluded coves and rocky outcrops. With the growth of coastal recreation and tourism, anthropogenic disturbance to pinnipeds – both on land and in water – is of increasing concern. Pinnipeds also face additional pressures from climate change, including increased coastal erosion and more frequent and intense storms.

Over the years, a number of legal mechanisms have developed to offer protection to marine mammals in the UK, including through both wildlife and fisheries legislation. However, there is no single legal instrument in the UK that is specifically designed for marine mammals.

Long before the development of modern conservation law, cetaceans were recognised in British law as animals of significant royal interest. Under a long-standing prerogative doctrine, these species were classified as 'royal fish' – a designation which means that when found stranded or caught in UK waters, they become the property of the Crown.[4] The doctrine of royal fish continues to hold symbolic and procedural significance within the UK's legal landscape, reflecting its enduring presence.[5]

---

4 The doctrine of royal fish originates in medieval English common law. One of the earliest references appears in Henry de Bracton's 13th century treatise *De Legibus et Consuetudinibus Angliae* ("On the Laws and Customs of England"), which states that the King is entitled to whales and sturgeon taken in the sea or elsewhere in the realm. In the 18th century, William Blackstone's *Commentaries on the Laws of England* affirmed this principle, noting that "A tenth branch of the king's ordinary revenue, said to be grounded on the consideration of his guarding and protecting the seas from pirates and robbers, is the right to royal fish, which are whale and sturgeon: and these, when either thrown ashore, or caught near the coasts, are the property of the king, on account of their superior excellence. Indeed our ancestors seem to have entertained a very high notion of the importance of this right; it being the prerogative of the kings of Denmark and the dukes of Normandy; and from one of these it was probably derived to our princes. It is expressly claimed and allowed in the statute *de praerogativa regis* [of the king's prerogative]: and the most ancient treatises of law now extant make mention of it." (William Blackstone, *Commentaries on the Laws of England*, Vol I (Oxford, 1765)). Although originally developed in England, the doctrine applies across the UK today, albeit with jurisdictional distinctions. In England, Wales and Northern Ireland, the rights to royal fish are exercised on behalf of the Crown by the Receiver of the Wreck, an official of the Maritime and Coastguard Agency – anyone finding a cetacean stranded along the coastline is required to report it to this authority. In Scotland, ownership of royal fish is reserved to the Crown and managed by the Crown Estate Scotland, though in practice any such strandings are handled by the Scottish Marine Animal Stranding Scheme (SMASS).

5 While the Crown may retain ownership of stranded cetaceans under the doctrine, in practice, the actual process of accessing, sampling or studying dead cetaceans is governed by wildlife laws such as the Wildlife and Countryside Act 1981 and the Conservation of Habitats and Species Regulations 2017 (and the various Habitats Regulations in Scotland and Northern Ireland). In England and Wales, for example, the UK Cetacean Strandings Investigation Programme (CSIP) is authorised by Defra to undertake post-mortem examinations on dead stranded cetaceans. Their

The legal framework for marine mammals in the UK has therefore emerged from a complex framework of domestic statutes, assimilated EU law and devolved governance structures.[6] This patchwork of regulatory regimes varies considerably in scope, application and enforceability, creating disparities in implementation. For instance, a species' legal status may differ based on its habitat, migratory behaviour or interactions with regulated activities such as commercial fishing, offshore energy development or marine tourism.

Navigating this intricate legal landscape presents significant challenges. Practitioners, policymakers and advocates often grapple with the task of interpreting how overlapping laws apply to specific circumstances. The reliance on general environmental or fisheries legislation and associated guidance can hamper efforts to achieve coherent legal scrutiny, effective

---

work is facilitated by the Receiver of the Wreck, who acts on behalf of the Crown.

6 The UK is made up of four nations – England, Wales, Scotland and Northern Ireland – with a system of devolved government that delegate varying degrees of legislative power to each. Devolution began in earnest with the passing of the Scotland Act 1998, the Government of Wales Act 1998 (and later 2006) and the Northern Ireland Act 1998, which established legislatures and governments in each of those nations. Under this framework, much environmental protection, nature conservation and wildlife law is devolved to the Scottish Parliament, the Senedd Cymru (Welsh Parliament) and the Northern Ireland Assembly. Consequently, each jurisdiction has the authority to develop its own environmental and conservation legislation. This has led to divergence in legal approaches across the UK. For example, the Conservation of Habitats and Species Regulations 2017 (as amended) in England and Wales, the Conservation (Natural Habitats, &c.) Regulations 1994 (as amended) in Scotland and the Conservation (Natural Habitats, etc.) Regulations (Northern Ireland) 1995 (as amended). Similarly, while the Wildlife and Countryside Act 1981 applies across Great Britain (England, Wales and Scotland), its provisions have been amended and interpreted differently in England, Wales and Scotland, resulting in variations in species protection and enforcement provisions. Understanding this devolution is essential to navigating the legal frameworks governing marine mammals in the UK.

enforcement and informed public engagement that is appropriate to these unique species and their marine environment. This inevitably undermines the robustness of legal protections afforded to marine mammals, leaving them vulnerable to both emerging and persistent threats.

Recognising this critical gap, this book seeks to provide a structured, practical legal resource focussed specifically on marine mammals within UK law. It consolidates and clarifies the relevant legal frameworks, clearly explaining their connections to offences, protected areas, assessment, disturbance, fisheries interactions, captivity, capture and welfare. Each chapter anchors its analysis in current statutory provisions while highlighting areas of legal ambiguity and potential reform.

By offering a comprehensive examination of the legal landscape, this book aims to enhance understanding and provide a unique resource for those seeking to reconcile marine mammals and law.

CHAPTER ONE

UNDERSTANDING OFFENCES AGAINST MARINE MAMMALS: NAVIGATING A FRAGMENTED LEGAL FRAMEWORK

INTRODUCTION

Marine mammal protections in the UK stem from international, European and domestic law.

All cetacean species found in UK waters are European protected species, being listed in Annex IV(a) of the EU Habitats Directive.[1] In addition, in England, Wales and Scotland, some cetaceans are nationally protected species, being listed in Schedule 5 of the Wildlife and Countryside Act 1981[2] (as amended) (**WCA 1981**). This dual status ostensibly offers strict protection against deliberate or reckless acts such as killing, injury or disturbance.

By contrast, pinniped protections are far less comprehensive. Neither the grey seal nor the harbour seal is listed in Annex IV(a) of the Habitats Directive and therefore neither species qualifies as a European protected species. The grey and harbour seal are also not included in Schedule 5 of the WCA 1981 in England, Wales and Scotland, meaning they lack full national protection under that instrument. Notably, the walrus is the only pinniped listed in Schedule 5 of the WCA 1981. In Northern

---

1 Council Directive 92/43/EEC of 21 May 1992 on the conservation of natural habitats and of wild fauna and flora.

2 Wildlife and Countryside Act 1981, c. 69.

Ireland however, pinnipeds are protected under the Wildlife (Northern Ireland) Order 1985 (as amended).[3]

Nevertheless, grey and harbour seals benefit from partial protections under other legislative instruments in England, Wales and Scotland, including the Conservation of Seals Act 1970[4] (as amended) and the Marine (Scotland) Act 2010.[5] Seals may also be protected when they form part of the notified features of Sites of Special Scientific Interest (**SSSIs.**[6]

The following statutes establish specific offences related to marine mammals in UK waters:

- The Conservation of Habitats and Species Regulations 2017,[7] as amended (applicable in England and Wales, including the adjacent territorial sea, up to 12 nautical miles (nm)[8] from the coastal baseline);[9]

- The Conservation of Offshore Marine Habitats and Species Regulations 2017,[10] as amended (applicable beyond 12nm

---

3 The Wildlife (Northern Ireland) Order 1985, No. 171 (N.I.2).

4 Conservation of Seals Act 1970, c. 30.

5 Marine (Scotland) Act 2010, asp. 5.

6 WCA 1981, section 28P.

7 The Conservation of Habitats and Species Regulations 2017, SI 2017/1012.

8 A nautical mile equals 1,852 metres.

9 The Conservation of Habitats and Species Regulations 2017 also extends and applies to Scotland and Northern Ireland (including the adjacent territorial sea to a limited degree), as regards reserved and excepted matters respectively. This is set out in regulation 2 of the Conservation of Habitats and Species Regulations 2017.

10 The Conservation of Offshore Marine Habitats and Species Regulations 2017, SI 2017/1013.

throughout the UK offshore marine area, including Scottish and Northern Irish offshore waters);[11]

- The Conservation (Natural Habitats, &c.) Regulations 1994,[12] as amended (applicable up to 12nm in Scottish inshore waters);[13]

- The Wildlife and Countryside Act 1981, as amended (applicable up to 12nm in England, Wales and Scotland);[14]

- The Conservation of Seals Act 1970, as amended (applicable up to 12nm in England and Wales);[15]

---

11 The Conservation of Offshore Marine Habitats and Species Regulations 2017 apply to the UK's offshore marine area, which means any part of the seabed and subsoil situated in any area designated under section 1(7) of the Continental Shelf Act 1964, and any part of the waters within British fishery limits (except the internal waters of, and the territorial sea adjacent to, the UK, the Channel Islands and the Isle of Man). This is broadly, beyond 12 nm from the coastal baseline and out to 200nm (Regulation 2(1), and Explanatory Memorandum to these Regulations, paragraphs 4.1 and 5),

12 The Conservation (Natural Habitats, &c.) Regulations 1994, SSI 1994/2716.

13 Referred to as the "Scottish marine area" which is defined as "the area of sea within the seaward limits of the territorial sea of the United Kingdom adjacent to Scotland" (regulation 2(1) of The Conservation (Natural Habitats, &c.) Regulations 1994).

14 The provisions of Part I of the WCA 1981 (which is relevant to Chapter 1 of this book) extends to the territorial waters adjacent to Great Britain, and for the purposes of Part 1, any part of Great Britain which is bounded by territorial waters shall be taken to include the territorial waters adjacent to that part (section 27(5) WCA 1981).

15 Section 17(2) and (3) of the Conservation of Seals Act 1970 state as follows: *"(2) Nothing done outside the seaward limits of the territorial waters adjacent to Great Britain shall constitute an offence under this Act. (3) This Act shall not extend to Northern Ireland."* The Conservation of Seals Act 1970 has been

- The Marine (Scotland) Act 2010 (applicable up to 12 nm in Scotland);[16]
- The Wildlife (Northern Ireland) Order 1985, as amended (applicable up to 12nm in Northern Ireland);[17] and
- The Conservation (Natural Habitats, etc) Regulations (Northern Ireland) 1995, as amended (applicable up to 12nm in Northern Ireland).[18]

Each of these legislative instruments contains varying definitions and thresholds for activities which constitute an offence – particularly regarding 'disturbance'[19] – and apply differently across UK jurisdictions due to devolution and legal divergence following the UK's withdrawal from the European Union (**Brexit**). These issues collectively create a fragmented and often incoherent legal landscape, as highlighted by the Environment, Food and Rural Affairs Committee in its 2023 report on marine mammal protection[20] (which is discussed in Chapter 9).

---

repealed in Scotland by virtue of section 130 of the Marine (Scotland) Act 2010.

16 The Marine (Scotland) Act 2010 applies to the "Scottish marine area", which is defined as the area of sea within the seaward limits of the territorial sea of the UK adjacent to Scotland and includes the bed and subsoil of the sea within that area (section 1(1) of the Marine (Scotland) Act 2010).

17 Article 2(5) of The Wildlife (Northern Ireland) Order 1985.

18 The Conservation (Natural Habitats, etc.) Regulations (Northern Ireland) 1995, SR 1995/380, regulation 2(4). Please note that only the original version (as it was originally made) is available on gov.uk. In order to view the amendments, please visit Westlaw.

19 Disturbance is discussed in further detail in Chapter 6.

20 House of Commons Environment, Food and Rural Affairs Committee, *Protecting Marine Mammals in the UK and Abroad*, Sixth Report of Session

This chapter provides an overview of these legal frameworks that govern offences against marine mammals in the UK, focussing on the different regimes for cetacean and pinniped species.

CETACEANS

European Protected Species

The Habitats Directive requires Member States to ensure the conservation of natural habitats and of wild species of fauna and flora of European Community Interest, aiming to maintain or restore them to 'favourable conservation status'.[21] In doing so, the Habitats Directive

---

2022-23, HC 697, Published on 28 June 2023 by authority of the House of Commons.

[21] The concept of favourable conservation status is fundamental to the Habitats Directive and underpins the objectives of both site-based and wider species protection measures. Article 1 of the Habitats Directive defines "conservation" as a series of measures required to maintain or restore natural habitats and species at a favourable status. Article 1(e) states that the conservation status of a natural habitat means the sum of the influences acting on a natural habitat and its typical species that may affect its long-term natural distribution, structure and functions as well as the long-term survival of its typical species; and that the conservation status of a natural habitat will be taken as 'favourable' when: its natural range and areas it covers within that range are stable or increasing; and the specific structure and functions which are necessary for its long-term maintenance exist and are likely to continue to exist for the foreseeable future; and the conservation status of its typical species is favourable, as defined in Article 1(i). Article 1(i) states that the conservation status of a species means the sum of the influences acting on the species concerned that may affect the long-term distribution and abundance of its populations within the territory, and that the conservation status will be taken as 'favourable' when: population dynamics data on the species concerned indicate that it is maintaining itself on a long-term basis as a viable component of its natural habitats; and the natural range of the species is neither being reduced nor is likely to be reduced for the foreseeable future; and there is, and will probably continue

obliges Member States to enforce a system of strict protection for species listed in Annex IV(a), which includes all cetaceans.[22]

Despite Brexit, the Habitats Directive remains embedded in domestic law[23] through:[24]

- The Conservation of Habitats and Species Regulations 2017, as amended;
- The Conservation of Offshore Marine Habitats and Species Regulations 2017, as amended;
- The Conservation (Natural Habitats, &c.) Regulations 1994, as amended; and
- The Conservation (Natural Habitats, etc) Regulations (Northern Ireland) 1995, as amended.

Where discussed together, these implementing Regulations are referred to as the '**various Habitats Regulations**' throughout this book. Where discussed individually, unless specified, reference is always to the most recent 'amended' version of the respective Regulations.

---

to be, a sufficiently large habitat to maintain its populations on a long-term basis.

22 The Mediterranean Monk Seal (*Monachus monachus*) is the only pinniped species listed in Annex IV(a) of the Habitats Directive. This species has never been recorded in UK waters. Accordingly, it is not discussed in this book.

23 And it will remain this way until the Government decides to reform it.

24 These regulations had to be updated to ensure that they continued to operate effectively following Brexit. Most of these changes involved transferring functions from the European Commission to the appropriate authorities, and all other processes or terms in the respective regulations currently remain unchanged and the existing guidance is still relevant.

'Strict Protection'

The key provision underpinning the legal protection of cetaceans is Article 12 of the Habitats Directive. Article 12 requires Member States to take requisite measures to establish a system of strict protection for Annex IV(a) species in their natural range, prohibiting, as applicable to marine mammals:

- all forms of deliberate capture or killing of specimens of these species in the wild;[25]
- deliberate disturbance of these species, particularly during the period of breeding, rearing, hibernation and migration;[26] and
- deterioration or destruction of breeding sites or resting places.[27]

In addition, Member States must establish a system to monitor the incidental capture and killing of Annex IV(a) species, and in light of the information gathered, undertake further research or conservation measures as required to ensure that incidental capture and killing does not have a significant negative impact on the species concerned.[28] This provision is discussed further in Chapter 7 on bycatch.

Offences under the various Habitats Regulations

The various Habitats Regulations implement the Habitats Directive with jurisdictional differences across England, Wales, Scotland and Northern Ireland.

---

25 Habitats Directive, Article 12(1)(a).

26 Habitats Directive, Article 12(1)(b).

27 Habitats Directive, Article 12(1)(d).

28 Habitats Directive, Article 12(4).

England and Wales

Under the Conservation of Habitats and Species Regulations 2017, it is an offence to deliberately capture, injure, kill[29] or disturb[30] wild animals of any species listed in Annex IV(a) of the Habitats Directive. Importantly, the 2017 Regulations provide a definition of 'disturbance of animals' (see Chapter 6 for more detail). This definition includes, in particular, any disturbance which is likely to impair their ability to survive, to breed or reproduce, to rear or nurture their young, to hibernate or migrate or to affect significantly the local distribution or abundance of the species to which they belong.[31]

The Conservation of Offshore Marine Habitats and Species Regulations 2017 broadly mirrors the suite of offences and the definition of 'disturbance', ensuring continuity of protection for cetaceans throughout UK offshore waters.[32]

Table 1 provides a summary of the offences under regulation 43 of the Conservation of Habitats and Species Regulations 2017 as applicable to marine mammals.

---

29 The Conservation of Habitats and Species Regulations 2017, regulation 43(1)(a).

30 The Conservation of Habitats and Species Regulations 2017, regulation 43(1)(b).

31 The Conservation of Habitats and Species Regulations 2017, regulation 43(2).

32 The Conservation of Offshore Marine Habitats and Species Regulations 2017, regulations 45(1) and (2) apply in the 'offshore marine area' of the UK, as per regulation 39(1).

Table 1 – Offences under regulation 43 of the Conservation of Habitats and Species Regulations 2017 as applicable to marine mammals

Offence	Jurisdiction	Whale	Dolphin	Porpoise	Pinniped
Reg 43(1)(a) – deliberately capture, injure or kill any wild animal of a European protected species.	E & W (up to 12 nm)	Yes	Yes	Yes	No
Reg 43(1)(b) – deliberately disturb wild animals of a European protected species. Under reg 43(2), for the purposes of the offence under reg 43(1)(b), disturbance of animals includes in particular any disturbance which is likely – (a) to impair their ability – (i) to survive, to breed or reproduce, or to rear or nurture their young; or (ii) in the case of animals of a hibernating or migratory species, to hibernate or migrate; or (b) to affect significantly the local distribution or abundance of the species to which they belong.	E & W (up to 12 nm)	Yes	Yes	Yes	No
Reg 43(1)(d) – damage or destroy a breeding site or resting place of a European protected species.	E & W (up to 12 nm)	Yes	Yes	Yes	No

Offence	Jurisdiction	Whale	Dolphin	Porpoise	Pinniped
Reg 43(3) (a) to be in possession of, or to control, (b) to transport, (c) to sell or exchange, (d) to offer for sale or exchange Reg 43(4) states that reg 43(3) applies to – (a) any live or dead animal or part of an animal – (i) which has been taken from the wild, and (ii) which is of a species or subspecies listed in Annex IV(a); and (b) anything derived from such an animal or any part of such an animal.	E & W (up to 12 nm)	Yes	Yes	Yes	No

Table 2 provides a summary of the offences under regulation 45 of the Conservation of Offshore Marine Habitats and Species Regulations 2017 as applicable to marine mammals.

Table 2 – Offences under regulation 45 of the Conservation of Offshore Marine Habitats and Species Regulations 2017 as applicable to marine mammals

Offence	Jurisdiction	Whale	Dolphin	Porpoise	Pinniped
Reg 45(1)(a) – deliberately capture, injure or kill any wild animal of a European protected species	E, W, S and NI offshore waters from 12nm to 200nm	Yes	Yes	Yes	No
Reg 45(1)(b) – deliberately disturb wild animals of a European protected species. Under reg 45(2), for the purposes of regulation 45(1)(b), disturbance of animals include in particular any disturbance which is likely – (a) to impair their ability – (i) to survive, to breed or reproduce, or to rear or nurture their young; or (ii) in the case of animals of a hibernating or migratory species, to hibernate or migrate; or (b) to affect significantly the local distribution or abundance of the species to which they belong.	E, W, S and NI offshore waters from 12nm to 200nm	Yes	Yes	Yes	No

Offence	Jurisdiction	Whale	Dolphin	Porpoise	Pinniped
Reg 45(1)(d) – damage or destroy, or do anything to cause the deterioration of, a breeding site or resting place of such an animal.	E, W, S and NI offshore waters from 12nm to 200nm	Yes	Yes	Yes	No
Reg 45(3) (a) to keep or transport (b) to sell or exchange, or (c) to offer for sale or exchange Under reg 45(4), reg 45(3) applies to (a) any live or dead animal or part of an animal – (i) which has been taken from the wild; and (ii) which is of a species or subspecies listed in Annex IV(a) to the Habitats Directive; and (b) any part of, or anything derived from, such an animal or any such part of an animal.	E, W, S and NI offshore waters from 12nm to 200nm	Yes	Yes	Yes	No

Scotland

Within Scottish territorial waters (up to 12nm), the relevant legislation is The Conservation (Natural Habitats, &c.) Regulations 1994, as amended. These Regulations also implement Article 12 of the Habitats Directive, but with different wording to that in English and Welsh territorial waters – for example, it is an offence to *deliberately or recklessly* capture, injure, kill, disturb or *harass* any cetacean.[33]

The inclusion of "recklessly" represents a broader mental element than in other parts of the UK and reflects Scotland's distinct approach to criminal liability in environmental law.

Table 3 provides a summary of the offences under regulation 39 of The Conservation (Natural Habitats, &c.) Regulations 1994 as applicable to marine mammals.

Table 3 – Offences under regulation 39 of the Conservation (Natural Habitats, &c.) Regulations 1994 as applicable to marine mammals

Offence	Jurisdiction	Whale	Dolphin	Porpoise	Pinniped
Reg 39(1)(a) – deliberately or recklessly capture, injure or kill a wild animal of a European protected species.	S (up to 12 nm)	Yes	Yes	Yes	No
Reg 39(1)(b) – deliberately or recklessly – (i) to harass a wild animal or group of wild animals of a European protected species; (ii) to disturb such an animal while it is occupying a structure or place which it uses for shelter or protection;	S (up to 12 nm)	Yes	Yes	Yes	No

33 The Conservation (Natural Habitats, &c.) Regulations 1994, regulations 39(1) and (2).

Offence	Jurisdiction	Whale	Dolphin	Porpoise	Pinniped
(iii) to disturb such an animal while it is rearing or otherwise caring for its young; (iv) to obstruct access to a breeding site or resting place of such an animal, or otherwise to deny the animal use of the breeding site or resting place; (v) to disturb such an animal in a manner that is, or in circumstances which are, likely to significantly affect the local distribution or abundance of the species to which it belongs; (vi) to disturb such an animal in a manner that is, or in circumstances which are, likely to impair its ability to survive, breed or reproduce, or rear or otherwise care for its young; or (vii) to disturb such an animal while it is migrating or hibernating.					
Reg 39(1)(d) – to damage or destroy a breeding site or resting place of such an animal.	S (up to 12 nm)	Yes	Yes	Yes	No
Reg 39(2) – deliberately or recklessly disturb any dolphin, porpoise or whale (cetacean)	S (up to 12 nm)	Yes	Yes	Yes	No

Offence	Jurisdiction	Whale	Dolphin	Porpoise	Pinniped
Reg 39(3) – (a) on or after 1 May 2007 to possess or control; (b) on or after 1 May 2007 to transport; (c) to sell or exchange; or (d) to offer for sale or exchange Under reg 39(4), reg 39(3) applies to (a) any live or dead animal or part of an animal – (i) which has been taken from the wild; and (ii) which is of a species or subspecies listed in Annex IV(a) to the Habitats Directive; and (b) anything derived from, such an animal or part of such an animal.	S (up to 12 nm)	Yes	Yes	Yes	No

Northern Ireland

Within Northern Irish territorial waters, The Conservation (Natural Habitats, etc) Regulations (Northern Ireland) 1995, as amended[34] implement Article 12 of the Habitats Directive, making it an offence to deliberately capture, injure or kill[35] a cetacean, or to deliberately disturb a cetacean while it is occupying a structure or place which it uses for

[34] Please note that the amendments are not available on Gov.uk. To view the most up to date version, please visit Westlaw.

[35] The Conservation (Natural Habitats, etc.) Regulations (Northern Ireland), regulation 34(1)(a).

shelter or protection.[36] It is also an offence to deliberately disturb such an animal in such a way as to be likely to[37]—

(i) affect the local distribution or abundance of the species to which it belongs;

(ii) impair its ability to survive, breed or reproduce, or rear or care for its young; or

(iii) impair its ability to hibernate or migrate.

Finally, it is also an offence to deliberately obstruct access to a cetacean's breeding site or resting place, or to damage or destroy their breeding site or resting place.[38]

Table 4 provides a summary of the offences under regulation 34 of the Conservation (Natural Habitats, etc.) Regulations (Northern Ireland) 1995, as amended, as applicable to marine mammals.

---

[36] The Conservation (Natural Habitats, etc.) Regulations (Northern Ireland), regulation 34(1)(b).

[37] The Conservation (Natural Habitats, etc.) Regulations (Northern Ireland), regulation 34(1)(c).

[38] The Conservation (Natural Habitats, etc.) Regulations (Northern Ireland), regulations 34(1)(e) and (f).

Table 4 – Offences under regulation 34 of the Conservation (Natural Habitats, etc.) Regulations (Northern Ireland) 1995 as applicable to marine mammals

Offence	Jurisdiction	Whale	Dolphin	Porpoise	Pinniped
Reg 34(1) (a) deliberately to capture, injure or kill a wild animal of a European protected species; (b) Deliberately to disturb any such animal while it is occupying a structure or place which it uses for shelter or protection; (c) deliberately to disturb such an animal in such a way as to be likely to— (i) affect the local distribution or abundance of the species to which it belongs; (ii) impair its ability to survive, breed or reproduce, or rear or care for its young; or (iii) impair its ability to hibernate or migrate; (d) … (e) deliberately to obstruct access to a breeding site or resting place of such an animal; or	NI (up to 12nm)	Yes	Yes	Yes	No

Offence	Jurisdiction	Whale	Dolphin	Porpoise	Pinniped
(f) to damage or destroy a breeding site or resting place of such an animal.					
Reg 34(2) – (a) to have in their possession or control; (b) to transport; (c) to sell or exchange, or (d) to offer for sale or exchange, any live or dead wild animal of a European protected species, or any part of, or anything derived from, such an animal.	NI (up to 12nm)	Yes	Yes	Yes	No

Together, the various Habitats Regulations provide a relatively coherent legal framework for the protection of cetaceans in UK waters, with offences across all UK jurisdictions, but with important variations in language and scope that practitioners and regulators must navigate carefully.

Offences under the Wildlife and Countryside Act 1981

The WCA 1981[39] applies to the territorial waters of England, Wales and Scotland and offers a separate layer of protection under national law for wildlife. However, the application of its provisions to cetaceans differs

[39] Wildlife and Countryside Act 1981, section 9 sets out the offences relating to certain wild animals listed in Schedule 5.

notably between England, Wales and Scotland due to legislative amendments over time.

England and Wales

All cetaceans are listed in Schedule 5 of the WCA 1981 in England and Wales. However, following amendments made by the Conservation (Natural Habitats, &c.) (Amendment) Regulations 2007[40], not all section 9 offences apply to all cetaceans. Specifically, sections 9(1) and 9(2) – which make it an offence to intentionally kill, injure or take a Schedule 5 species, or to be in possession or control of any live or dead animal, or part of, or anything derived from such an animal – no longer apply to cetaceans.

In addition, section 9(4A) WCA 1981 – the offence of intentionally or recklessly disturbing certain species – only applies to whale and dolphin species. Notably, it does not apply to the harbour porpoise.

However, section 9(5) WCA 1981 applies to all cetaceans. This is the offence of selling, offering or exposing for sale, or having in possession or transporting for the purpose of sale, any live or dead wild animal, or any part of, or anything derived from such an animal; or publishing or causing to be published, any advertisement likely to be understood as conveying that he buys or sells, or intends to buy or sell any of those things.

---

40 The Conservation (Natural Habitats, &c.) (Amendment) Regulations 2007, SI 2007/1843, regulation 7(7)(f), (g) and (h).

Scotland

In Scotland, the WCA 1981 was amended by the Conservation (Natural Habitats, &c.) Amendment (Scotland) Regulations 2007,[41] which removed all cetaceans from Schedule 5. As a result, none of the offences in section 9 WCA 1981 apply to cetaceans.

Table 5 provides a summary of the offences under section 9 WCA 1981 as applicable to marine mammals.

Table 5 – Offences under section 9 Wildlife and Countryside Act 1981 as applicable to marine mammals

Offence	**Jurisdiction**	**Whale**	**Dolphin**	**Porpoise**	**Pinniped**[42]
S9(1) – intentionally kill, injure or take	E & W	No	No	No	Walrus only
S9(1) – intentionally or recklessly kill, injure or take	S	No	No	No	Walrus only

[41] In Scotland, all cetaceans were removed from Schedule 5 by section 28 of The Conservation (Natural Habitats, &c.) Amendment (Scotland) Regulations 2007/80. However, the WCA 1981 in Scotland still includes the offence in section 9(4A) of intentionally or recklessly, disturbing or harassing any cetacean. It appears that section 9(4A), which was added in 2004, was not updated to reflect the removal of all cetaceans from Schedule 5 in 2007. Please note that on the gov.uk version of the WCA 1981, two species of cetacean remain listed in Schedule 5 – *Tursiops truncatus* and *Delphinus delphis* – however, these species are not listed on Westlaw. This is inevitably confusing to a reader of the gov.uk version, and therefore footnote C1 must be pointed out – this reiterates that all dolphins and porpoises are removed by the Regulations, but that the text has not been altered.

[42] Please see the following section of Chapter 1 for commentary on Pinnipeds and in particular, the walrus.

Offence	Jurisdiction	Whale	Dolphin	Porpoise	Pinniped[42]
S9(2) – has in their possession or control any live or dead wild animal or any part of, or anything derived from, such an animal	E, W & S	No	No	No	Walrus only
S9(4) – intentionally or recklessly – (a) damages or destroys any structure or place which any wild animal uses for shelter or protection; (b) disturbs any such animal while it is occupying a structure or place which it uses for shelter or protection; or (c) obstructs access to any structure or place which any such animal uses for shelter or protection.	E & W	No	No	No	Walrus only
S9(4) – intentionally or recklessly – (a) damages or destroys, or obstructs access to, any structure or place which any wild animal uses for shelter or protection; or (b) disturbs any such animal while it is occupying a structure or place which it uses for that purpose.	S	No	No	No	Walrus only

Offence	Jurisdiction	Whale	Dolphin	Porpoise	Pinniped[42]
S9(4A)(a) – intentionally or recklessly disturbs a dolphin or whale (cetacea)	E & W	Yes	Yes	No	N/A
S9(4A)(a) – intentionally or recklessly disturbs or harasses any wild animal in Schedule 5 as a dolphin, whale or porpoise (cetacea)	S	No	No	No	N/A
S9(5) (a) sells, offers or exposes for sale, or has in their possession or transports for the purposes of sale, any live or dead wild animal, or any part of, or anything derived from, such an animal; or (b) publishes or causes to be published any advertisement likely to be understood as conveying that they buy or sell, or intends to buy or sell, any of those things	E & W	Yes	Yes	Yes	Walrus only
S9(5) (a) sells, offers or exposes for sale, or has in his possession or transports for the purpose of sale, any live or dead wild animal, or any part of, or anything derived from, such an animal; or	S	No	No	No	Walrus only

Offence	Jurisdiction	Whale	Dolphin	Porpoise	Pinniped[42]
(b) publishes or causes to be published any advertisement likely to be understood as conveying that he buys or sells, or intends to buy or sell, any of those things					
S9(5A) – knowingly causes or permits to be done an act which is made unlawful by any of the foregoing provisions of this section (other than subsection (5)(b))	S	No	No	No	Walrus only

Northern Ireland

The Wildlife (Northern Ireland) Order 1985 does not apply to cetaceans – all cetaceans were removed from Schedule 5 by virtue of the Conservation (Natural Habitats, etc) (Amendment) Regulations (Northern Ireland) 2007.[43] The Explanatory Memorandum to these Regulations explains that regulation 38 removes references to European protected species from the Wildlife (Northern Ireland) Order 1985.

Summary of the complexities and inconsistencies for cetaceans

The legal framework for the protection of cetaceans in the UK is marked by a number of complexities and inconsistencies, particularly when comparing the primary national legislation – the WCA 1981 and the Wildlife (Northern Ireland) Order 1995, with the various Habitats Regulations. As outlined above, the offences under the national

[43] The Conservation (Natural Habitats, etc) (Amendment) Regulations (Northern Ireland) 2007, S.R. 2007/345, regulation 38(a).

legislation are not aligned with those under the various Habitats Regulations, resulting in divergent levels of protection depending on species, location and legal instrument.

A key source of inconsistency stems from the differing application of legal protections to different cetacean species across the UK jurisdictions. For example, under the WCA 1981 in England and Wales, only whales and dolphins benefit from the offence under section 9(4A) (intentionally or recklessly disturbing), leaving the harbour porpoise without coverage under this provision. In Scotland, no cetaceans are afforded protection under section 9 WCA 1981. In Northern Ireland, no cetaceans are afforded protection under section 10 of the Wildlife (Northern Ireland) Order 1985.

The 2007 amendments to the WCA 1981 and to the Wildlife (Northern Ireland) Order 1985, which removed or restricted the applicability of offences to cetaceans, have thus created a situation where the primary pieces of UK wildlife legislation no longer afford a full suite of protection to cetaceans. Instead, the protection of cetaceans now relies almost entirely on the various Habitats Regulations.

These various Habitats Regulations are assimilated EU law (formerly referred to as retained EU law), and as such they do not carry the same legal status or permanence as primary legislation. Since Brexit, assimilated EU law has also become more vulnerable to amendment or repeal, particularly under provisions introduced by the Environment Act 2021,[44] the Retained EU Law (Revocation and Reform) Act 2023,[45] the Energy Act 2023[46] and possible forthcoming provisions as a result of the Levelling Up and Regeneration Act 2023 and the Planning and Infrastructure Bill. This raises real concern about the durability and consistency of cetacean protection in the longer term, particularly as the

44 Environment Act 2021, c. 30, section 112.

45 Retained EU Law (Revocation and Reform) Act 2023, c. 28.

46 Energy Act 2023, c. 52.

WCA 1981 and the Wildlife (Northern Ireland) Order 1985 no longer provides a full and independent domestic safeguard for these species.

In summary, the legal framework for offences against cetaceans in the UK is fragmented, with varying degrees of protection across jurisdictions, a dependence on secondary legislation and a lack of coherence between statutory regimes. This fragmentation not only creates uncertainty for regulators and developers but also undermines effective conservation and enforcement efforts.

PINNIPEDS

Pinniped species – namely grey seals, harbour seals, and the vagrant walrus – are also subject to a fragmented and incoherent legal regime throughout the UK. The legal protections afforded to these species vary considerably across jurisdictions and legislative instruments, and in many instances, are inadequate to prevent disturbance or harm. As noted above, UK pinniped species are not European protected species and therefore the provisions of the various Habitats Regulations, discussed above in relation to cetaceans, do not apply to them.

The Wildlife and Countryside Act 1981

The only pinniped species listed in Schedule 5 of the WCA 1981 is the walrus, a vagrant species that occasionally visits UK waters. This means that resident pinniped species – grey and harbour seals – do not receive protection under section 9 WCA 1981, which prohibits acts such as killing, injuring or disturbing listed species.

As a result, in England, Wales and Scotland, it is not an offence under the WCA 1981 to intentionally or recklessly disturb a pinniped (other than the walrus). This creates a significant gap in legal protection, particularly in light of increasing human activity in coastal and marine environments.

Please refer to Table 5 above to view how the WCA 1981 applies to the walrus.

Other national legal regimes

Beyond the WCA 1981, the principal legislation governing seals in England and Wales is the Conservation of Seals Act 1970 (as amended).[47] Under the Conservation of Seals Act, it is an offence to intentionally or recklessly kill, injure or take a seal.[48] Further offences include attempts to commit such acts and the possession of firearms, explosives or poisonous substances for the purpose of committing them.[49] There are exceptions to these offences, including the taking or attempted taking of any seal which had been disabled and was taken solely for the purpose of tending it and releasing it when no longer disabled[50] or where the reason for killing a seal which had been so seriously disabled and had no reasonable chance of recovering.[51]

In July 2025, the Marine Management Organisation (**MMO**)[52] advised that the relocation of 'healthy' grey and common seals that are not in need of medical intervention is classed as 'taking' of seals under the Conservation of Seals Act 1970, for example, where a healthy seal is in a dangerous location such as a road, urban area or near heavy machinery. The MMO's guidance defines a healthy seal as one that is mobile and alert and shows no visible signs of injury or illness, and is not a dependent

---

47 The Conservation of Seals Act 1970 was repealed in Scotland by section 130 of the Marine (Scotland) Act 2010.

48 Conservation of Seals Act 1970, section 1.

49 Conservation of Seals Act 1970, section 8.

50 Conservation of Seals Act 1970, section 9(1)(a).

51 Conservation of Seals Act 1970, section 9(2).

52 Section 9(1) of the Marine and Coastal Access Act 2009 transferred the Secretary of State's functions of granting and revoking licences under section 10 of the Conservation of Seals Act 1970 to the MMO.

pup (i.e., it has been weaned and is capable of independent survival).[53] Therefore, it is unlawful to carry out this activity without a licence. As of the date of the law in this book, licensing has only been implemented for England, though it is anticipated that the other jurisdictions will follow suit soon.

However, the Conservation of Seals Act 1970 presents several difficulties: It contains no definition of "seal", raising interpretive questions about its scope and applicability, particularly regarding whether it extends to pinniped species beyond grey and harbour seals. It also contains no offence of disturbance, nor any provisions addressing the harassment of seals at sea or on land, including at haul-out sites.

In Scotland, the Marine (Scotland) Act 2010 makes it an offence to intentionally or recklessly kill, injure or take a live seal.[54] However, like the Conservation of Seals Act 1970, the term "seal" is not defined.

Limited and jurisdiction-specific disturbance protections

Some limited legal protection from disturbance is available to pinnipeds under other legal frameworks, although these are both geographically and contextually constrained.

First, disturbance of seals may constitute an offence where they are a notified special interest feature of a Site of Special Scientific Interest.[55] However, this protection is highly site-specific and does not offer a general prohibition on disturbance (this is discussed further in Chapter 2 on protected sites).

53 https://marinedevelopments.blog.gov.uk/2025/07/09/why-you-need-a-wildlife-licence-to-move-a-healthy-seal/ (accessed on 31 July 2025)

54 Marine (Scotland) Act 2010, section 107.

55 Wildlife and Countryside Act 1981, section 28P.

Second, in Scotland, it is an offence to intentionally or recklessly harass a seal at a designated haul-out site.[56] However, its application is limited to locations formally designated by Scottish Ministers. The Protection of Seals (Designation of Haul-Out Sites) (Scotland) Order 2014[57] identified 194 such sites, with amendments in 2017 adding one further location.[58]

The Wildlife (Northern Ireland) Order 1985

Article 10 of the Wildlife (Northern Ireland) Order 1985 sets out a number of offences applicable to all animals listed in Schedule 5, which includes seals (defined in the Order as "pinnipeds").[59] These offences include intentionally or recklessly killing, injuring or taking a pinniped[60]; and intentionally or recklessly – damaging or destroying, or obstructing access to, any structure or place which a pinniped uses for shelter or protection,[61] damaging or destroying anything which conceals or protects such a structure,[62] or disturbing a seal when it is occupying a structure or place used for shelter or protection.[63] It is also an offence to intentionally or recklessly disturb a pinniped.[64] In addition, a person commits an

56 Marine (Scotland) Act 2010, section 117.

57 The Protection of Seals (Designation of Haul-Out Sites) (Scotland) Order 2014, SSI 2014/185.

58 The Protection of Seals (Designation of Haul-Out Sites) (Scotland) Amendment Order 2017, SSI 2017/63.

59 The Fisheries Act 2020, section 54(2) and Schedule 9, paragraph 17 expanded this from only the grey and harbour (common) seal, to include all pinnipeds.

60 The Wildlife (Northern Ireland) Order 1985, article 10(1)

61 The Wildlife (Northern Ireland) Order 1985, article 10(4)(a)

62 The Wildlife (Northern Ireland) Order 1985, article 10(4)(b).

63 The Wildlife (Northern Ireland) Order 1985, article 10(4)(c).

64 The Wildlife (Northern Ireland) Order 1985, article 10(4A)(a).

offence if they cause or knowingly permit any of the above unlawful acts to be done.[65]

Table 6 provides a summary of the offences under Article 10 of the Wildlife (Northern Ireland) Order 1985 as applicable to marine mammals.

Table 6 – Offences under Article 10 of the Wildlife (Northern Ireland) Order 1985 as applicable to marine mammals

Offence	Jurisdiction	Whale	Dolphin	Porpoise	Pinniped
Art 10(1) – intentionally or recklessly kill, injure or take	NI (up to 12nm)	No	No	No	Yes
Art 10(2) – have in their possession or control any live or dead wild animal or any part of, or anything derived from, such an animal	NI (up to 12nm)	No	No	No	Yes
Art 10(4) – intentionally or recklessly – (a) damages or destroys, or obstructs access to, any structure or place which any wild animal uses for shelter or protection; (b) damages or destroys anything which conceals or protects any such structure; or	NI (up to 12nm)	No	No	No	Yes

[65] The Wildlife (Northern Ireland) Order 1985, article 10(4B).

Offence	Jurisdiction	Whale	Dolphin	Porpoise	Pinniped
(c) disturbs any such animal while it is occupying a structure or place which it uses for shelter or protection					
Art 10(4A) – intentionally or recklessly disturbs (a) a seal (pinniped)	NI (up to 12nm)	No	No	No	Yes
Art 10(4B) – knowingly causes or permits to be done an act which is made unlawful by any of the foregoing provisions of Article 10	NI (up to 12nm)	No	No	No	Yes

Summary of the complexities and inconsistencies for pinnipeds

The laws for the protection of pinnipeds in the UK are fragmented across multiple instruments, each with differing geographical scopes, offence types and enforcement mechanisms. Notably:

- Resident pinnipeds in England, Wales and Scotland receive weaker protection than the vagrant walrus, which is afforded full protection under Schedule 5 WCA 1981;
- There is no harmonised offence of disturbance applicable to pinnipeds across the UK;
- The designation-based approach in Scotland excludes many haul-out sites due to inflexibility in statutory definitions; and
- Key legislative terms, such as “seal”, lack clarity for application, undermining enforcement and protection.

EXCEPTIONS AND STATUTORY DEFENCES

There are several exceptions and statutory defences available in relation to the offences discussed above. Chapters 6 (disturbance), 7 (bycatch) and 8 (capture) provide detailed information on these defences for each topic.

PENALTIES FOR OFFENCES AGAINST MARINE MAMMALS

The penalties for offences against marine mammals under UK law vary depending on the legislation and jurisdiction involved.

Under the WCA 1981, a person guilty of an offence under section 9 (which includes the offence in England and Wales under section 9(4A) of intentionally or recklessly disturbing a whale or dolphin) shall be liable on summary conviction to imprisonment for a term not exceeding six months or to a fine not exceeding level five on the standard scale, or to both.[66] Where the offence has been committed in respect of more than one animal, the maximum fine shall be determined as if the person convicted had been convicted of a separate offence in respect of each animal.[67]

Under the Wildlife (Northern Ireland) Order 1985, a person guilty of an offence under Article 10 shall be liable on summary conviction to imprisonment for a term not exceeding 6 months or to a fine not exceeding level 5 on the standard scale, or to both.[68] Where the offence has been committed in respect of more than one animal, the maximum

66 WCA 1981, section 21(1).

67 WCA 1981, section 21(5).

68 The Wildlife (Northern Ireland) Order 1985, Article 27(1)(a).

fine shall be determined as if the person convicted had been convicted of a separate offence in respect of each animal.[69]

Under the Conservation of Habitats and Species Regulations 2017, a person guilty of an offence under regulation 43 is liable on summary conviction to imprisonment for a term not exceeding six months or to a fine, or to both.[70]

Under the Conservation of Offshore Marine Habitats and Species Regulations 2017, a person guilty of an offence under regulation 45 is liable, either on summary conviction or on conviction on indictment, to a fine.[71]

In Scotland, under the Conservation (Natural Habitats, &c.) Regulations 1994, a person guilty of an offence under regulation 39 is liable (a) on summary conviction, to imprisonment for a term not exceeding 12 months or a fine not exceeding £40,000 (or both), (b) on conviction on indictment, to imprisonment for a term not exceeding 5 years or a fine (or both).[72]

In Northern Ireland, under the Conservation (Natural Habitats, etc.) Regulations (Northern Ireland) 1995, a person guilty of an offence under regulation 34 shall be liable on summary conviction to a fine not exceeding level 5 on the standard scale.[73]

69 The Wildlife (Northern Ireland) Order 1985, Article 27(7).

70 Conservation of Habitats and Species Regulations 2017, regulation 43(8).

71 Conservation of Offshore Marine Habitats and Species Regulations 2017, regulation 48.

72 The Conservation (Natural Habitats, &c.) Regulations 1994, regulation 39(12).

73 The Conservation (Natural Habitats, etc.) Regulations (Northern Ireland) 1995, regulation 34(11).

Under the Marine (Scotland) Act 2010, a person guilty of an offence under section 107 is liable (a) on summary conviction, to imprisonment for a term not exceeding 12 months or a fine not exceeding £40,000 (or both), (b) on conviction on indictment, to imprisonment for a term not exceeding 5 years or a fine (or both).[74] A person guilty of an offence under section 117 is liable, on summary conviction, to imprisonment for a term not exceeding six months or to a fine not exceeding level 5 on the standard scale, or to both.[75]

Under the Conservation of Seals Act 1970, a person guilty of an offence under section 1, 8 or 9 shall be liable on summary conviction to a fine not exceeding level 4 on the standard scale. [76]

CHALLENGES IN INTERPRETATION AND APPLICATION

Even where legal protections for marine mammals exist under the various UK legal frameworks, challenges persist in the interpretation and application of these provisions. One of the most complex and often contested areas relates to the offence of 'disturbance' – which is discussed in Chapter 6. Defining what constitutes disturbance, and more importantly, evidencing it in practice, presents a major hurdle to effective enforcement.

Unlike some terrestrial species, there is limited guidance available for marine mammals to support regulators, developers or prosecutors in assessing when an offence has occurred. This is in stark contrast to terrestrial species such as bats, where a comparatively richer body of statutory guidance, technical protocols and licensing practices exist to

74 Marine (Scotland) Act 2010, section 128(A1).

75 Marine (Scotland) Act 2010, section 128(1).

76 Conservation of Seals Act, section 5(2).

interpret similar legal terms. This underscores the divide in practice between approaches to terrestrial and marine mammal species.

Compounding this challenge is the lack of case law and limited enforcement activity in the marine environment. There are very few recorded prosecutions relating to cetacean disturbance or other marine mammal offences under either the various Habitats Regulations or the primary national legislation. This creates uncertainty as to how the statutory language is applied in practice and leaves key legal questions – such as the thresholds for 'deliberate' or 'reckless' disturbance – unresolved. In addition, regulatory undertakings such as civil sanctions are not available for any protected species.

SUMMARY

The legal framework governing offences against marine mammals in the UK is complex, disjointed and jurisdictionally uneven. Across the different nations, the various statutes operate with differing scopes, thresholds and definitions – particularly in relation to disturbance – and offer inconsistent levels of protection depending on geography, species and legal instrument. These discrepancies are most acute in the divergence between cetacean and pinniped protections, and in the weakening of domestic primary legislation following legislative reforms in 2007. The result is a patchwork system in which meaningful protection relies heavily on assimilated EU law, which is now increasingly vulnerable to political and legislative change. In addition, this fragmentation further complicates enforcement and regulatory compliance.

CHAPTER TWO

PROTECTED SITES FOR MARINE MAMMALS

INTRODUCTION

In the UK, the designation of protected sites is a fundamental legal mechanism for the conservation of marine mammals. Under the Habitats Directive – now assimilated into UK law – several marine mammal species are listed as Annex II species, requiring the designation of Special Areas of Conservation (**SACs**). In UK waters, this includes sites designated for harbour porpoise, bottlenose dolphin, grey seal and harbour seal.

Designating protected sites for marine mammals presents significant challenges. These species are highly mobile, often traversing vast ranges including offshore and transboundary waters, defying our anthropocentric fixed boundaries. Nevertheless, following sustained legal pressure and litigation – including a 2018 judgment concerning the UK's failure to designate any SACs for harbour porpoise[1] – a network of marine mammal SACs has now been established. In addition, some Sites of Special Scientific Interest (**SSSIs**) list include seals and haul out sites in their citation.

This chapter outlines the legal framework governing the designation and management of protected sites for marine mammals.

1 *European Commission v United Kingdom of Great Britain and Northern Ireland*, Case C-669/16.

MARINE MAMMALS AS DESIGNATED FEATURES OF MARINE PROTECTED AREAS

Marine mammals as Annex II species under the Habitats Directive

Marine mammals are afforded varying levels of legal protection under the Habitats Directive – this includes not only strict protection under Article 12 for all cetaceans (discussed in Chapter 1), but also through the designation of protected sites – Special Areas of Conservation (**SACs**) for species listed in Annex II of the Habitats Directive, the regime for which is set out in Article 6 of the Habitats Directive. In the UK, this regime continues post-Brexit and the network of protected sites, including SACs, is referred to as the National Site Network.[2]

Marine mammal species listed in Annex II are:

- Grey seal
- Harbour seal
- Harbour porpoise
- Bottlenose dolphin
- Mediterranean monk seal[3]

Annex II species may also be listed in Annex IV(a) (as is the case for the harbour porpoise and bottlenose dolphin), which triggers a separate

---

[2] Throughout the European Union, this is referred to as the Natura 2000 network and is referred to as such in the Habitats Directive.

[3] The Mediterranean Monk Seal (*Monachus monachus*) has never been recorded in UK waters. Accordingly, it is not discussed further in this chapter.

system of strict protection under Article 12 (as discussed in Chapter 1). The dual listing creates overlapping obligations:

- Article 6 protects Annex II species through the designation and management of sites (SACs) and is therefore limited geographically in respect of those sites (and functionally linked areas) designated for such species.

- Article 12 protects individual animals and populations of all Annex IV(a) species (all cetaceans), throughout the natural range of the species, including outside of SACs, through prohibitions on deliberate capture, killing and disturbance.

Therefore, the harbour porpoise and bottlenose dolphin are afforded protection through both site designation (SACs) and through species-based protections across their entire range.

The UK has retained the requirement to designate SACs for Annex II species following Brexit.

Designating Special Areas of Conservation under the Habitats Directive

Articles 3 and 4 of the Habitats Directive provide the foundation for establishing SACs within the Natura 2000 / National Site Network.

Article 3 sets out the overarching objective: the creation of a "*coherent European ecological network*" of SACs, known as Natura 2000. This network must include sites that host the habitats of species listed in Annex II. The ultimate aim is to restore these habitats to a "favourable conservation status" across their natural range. Each Member State has a duty to contribute to this network proportionately, based on the presence of the relevant habitat types and species within its territory.

Article 4 details the procedural steps for SAC designation. Each Member State must use scientific information and the criteria in Annex III of the

Habitats Directive to compile a list of proposed sites. For Annex II species that range widely – such as marine mammals – proposed SACs must be those areas within the species' natural range that contain the physical and biological factors essential to their life and reproduction. In the case of widely ranging aquatic species, SACs must be clearly identifiable areas where these essential factors are present. States are also required to adapt their list of sites in light of the results of ongoing surveillance (as per Article 11 of the Habitats Directive).

Together, Articles 3 and 4 underscore the scientific and ecological rigour required in identifying SACs and highlight the duty on Member States, including the UK (whose obligations continue post-Brexit), to actively contribute to the conservation of marine mammal habitats through site-based protection mechanisms.

UK Special Areas of Conservation designated for marine mammals

Bottlenose dolphins

Soon after the Habitats Directive came into force, the UK designated two candidate SACs for bottlenose dolphins, which were approved – Cardigan Bay SAC in Wales and the Moray Firth SAC in Scotland.

The Joint Nature Conservation Committee (**JNCC**)[4] identifies Cardigan Bay and the Moray Firth as the only two areas in UK waters possessing the essential physical and biological conditions needed to support the only semi-resident populations of bottlenose dolphin. Therefore, these regions were subsequently designated as SACs. While dolphins from these sites may venture further afield seasonally, they are present year-

[4] The Joint Nature Conservation Committee (JNCC) is the statutory advisor to the UK government and devolved administrations on UK-wide and international nature conservation. As part of its role, JNCC provides scientific advice to the UK Government and devolved administrations on Marine Protected Areas (MPAs).

round in these sites, with individuals observed consistently over several years.[5]

In addition, the bottlenose dolphin is a qualifying feature, but not a primary reason for the site selection of the Pen Llyn a'r Sarnau / Lleyn Peninsula and the Sarnau SAC in Wales.

Harbour porpoise

The harbour porpoise has been at the centre of significant legal proceedings concerning the UK's obligations under the Habitats Directive to designate SACs for this species.[6]

The European Commission claimed in 2012 that the UK had failed to fulfil its obligations under Articles 3(2) and 4(1) and Annexes II and III of the Habitats Directive, in so far as those obligations concerned the protection of the harbour porpoise.[7] In accordance with those provisions, each Member State whose territory includes sites hosting the harbour porpoise was required to send the Commission a list of sites proposed for the protection of that species by 10 June 1995 at the latest. Given the complexity of creating a Natura 2000 network in the marine environment, formed of various SACs, the European Commission did not, initially, bring actions against Member States that did not meet this deadline. However, a Commission Notice published in May 2006[8] clarified that the Marine Natura 2000 network should be completed by 2012 at the latest. By that time, every other Member State hosting the

5 JNCC Guidance for bottlenose dolphin, available here: https://sac.jncc.gov.uk/species/S1349/

6 *European Commission v United Kingdom of Great Britain and Northern Ireland*, Case C-669/16.

7 Case C-669/16, paragraph 46.

8 Commission Notice (COM(2006) 2016 of 22 May 2006, *Halting the loss of biodiversity by 2010 – and beyond – Sustaining ecosystem services for human well-being.*

harbour porpoise had submitted proposed SACs, leaving the UK as the sole exception.

In 2012, the European Commission received a formal complaint from the non-governmental organisation World Wildlife Fund UK (**WWF**), which alleged that the UK had failed to designate SACs for the harbour porpoise, contrary to its legal obligations under the Habitats Directive. Accompanying the complaint was a report entitled "*Protecting the Harbour Porpoise in UK Seas*". This report identified six sites which it claimed should, on the basis of the scientific data available, be designated as SACs for harbour porpoise.

Following the complaint, and after assessing further information provided, the European Commission addressed a reasoned opinion to the UK in October 2014, charging it with failure to fulfil its obligation to propose, in accordance with Articles 3(2) and 4(1) of the Habitats Directive, a sufficient number of sites for the harbour porpoise. At that time, only one site had been formally proposed for designation by the UK. The European Commission also stated that it was concerned that one of the practical implications of the failure to fulfil this obligation, and, accordingly, the failure to afford those sites protection under Article 6 of the Habitats Directive, was that applications for offshore wind farms were being processed without due regard for the impact of those applications on the harbour porpoise populations.[9]

In December 2016, the European Commission initiated infringement proceedings against the UK before the Court of Justice of the European Union (**CJEU**), asserting that the UK had not taken the necessary measures to meet its obligations under the Habitats Directive. The European Commission argued that the UK's proposal of only one SAC for harbour porpoise was manifestly insufficient. It set out a number of grounds, including:

---

[9] Case C-669/16, paragraph 19.

1. approximately 56% of the harbour porpoise's range in the Atlantic biogeographic region falls within the UK marine waters, yet the UK had proposed only a single site which represented barely 0.1% of that area;[10]

2. the six sites identified in WWF's 2012 report were based on data that, in the Commission's view, should have led the UK to propose those sites as candidate SACs;[11] and

3. other Member States were able to designate sites for the harbour porpoise immediately adjacent to a site identified in the WWF 2012 report as warranting being proposed for designation as an SAC, but which the UK had failed to propose.[12]

In its defence, the UK submitted, first that the identification of suitable potential SACs for the harbour porpoise is an extremely difficult process, particularly in light of the express requirement in the Habitats Directive that sites should be proposed for SACs only if they are 'clearly identifiable', the need for a rigorous scientific assessment of the suitability of particular sites as potential SACs, and the imperative to avoid the vain expenditure of resources on sites that will not, as a matter of fact, contribute to the attainment of the aims of the Habitats Directive and the Natura 2000 network.[13] Nevertheless, the UK acknowledged that it had failed to meet its obligations as of the date of the reasoned opinion.[14]

The CJEU ruled against the UK on 17 October 2018, finding that the UK had failed to fulfil its obligations under Articles 3(2) and 4(1) of the Habitats Directive. The CJEU held that the UK had not proposed a sufficient number of SACs for the harbour porpoise and had failed to

---

10 Case C-669/16, paragraph 49.

11 Case C-669/16, paragraph 50.

12 Case C-669/16, paragraph 52.

13 Case C-669/16, paragraph 55.

14 Case C-669/16, paragraph 56.

contribute proportionately to the establishment of the Natura 2000 network.

In response, in 2019, the UK designated six SACs for harbour porpoise in its waters:[15]

- Bristol Channel Approaches SAC
- Inner Hebrides and the Minches SAC
- North Anglesey Marine SAC
- North Channel SAC
- Southern North Sea SAC
- West Wales Marine SAC

In addition, harbour porpoise is a qualifying feature, but not the primary reason for site selection, for the Skerries and Causeway SAC in Northern Ireland.

This high-profile litigation served as a landmark case on the obligations of EU Member States to designate marine SACs, and it underscored the role of scientific evidence, NGO advocacy and European Commission enforcement in achieving compliance with EU nature conservation law.

Harbour seals

The JNCC has stated that site selection has favoured sites that are important both as general haul-out sites and for moulting and pupping. The largest breeding colony has been selected, in the south of the species' range in the UK. The geographic range of breeding has been covered by

15 https://sac.jncc.gov.uk/species/S1351/

the selection of a representative sample of relatively large colonies in the north. Sites have been selected using the most up-to-date population data available, but populations at individual sites may fluctuate, with low numbers at many sites, meaning it can be difficult to define the boundaries of specific sites. Haul-out areas are thought to be very important for the conservation of the species, as are the most important breeding colonies. As well as their importance in maintaining overall population size, larger breeding sites are significant as sources of emigration to smaller or newly established colonies[16].

Sites where harbour seals are primary interest features are:

- Ascrib, Isay and Dunvegan SAC (north west Skye)
- Dornoch Firth and Morrich More SAC (north east Scotland)
- Eileanan agus Sgeiran Lios mor SAC (Island of Lismore, west Scotland)
- Firth of Tay and Eden Estuary SAC (east Scotland)
- Mousa SAC (Shetland)
- Sanday SAC (Orkney)
- South-East Islay Skerries SAC (Inner Hebrides)
- The Wash and North Norfolk Coast SAC (east England)
- Yell Sound Coast SAC (Shetland)

[16] https://sac.jncc.gov.uk/species/S1365/

In addition, at the following sites, harbour seals are a qualifying interest feature, but not a primary reason for site selection:

- Murlough SAC (Northern Ireland)
- Sound of Barra SAC (west Scotland)
- Strangford Lough SAC (Northern Ireland)

Grey seals

According to the JNCC, site selection rationale for grey seals takes account of the UK's special responsibility to protect this species. The largest breeding colonies, based on pup production, have been selected. Sites have been identified using the most up-to-date population data available, although populations at individual sites may fluctuate. Colonies have also been selected to ensure coverage of the geographical range of breeding in the UK. The sites selected contain a significant proportion of the UK breeding population of grey seals.[17]

Sites where grey seals are primary features are:

- Berwickshire and North Northumberland Coast SAC (east England and Scotland)
- Faray and Holm of Faray SAC (Orkney)
- Isle of May SAC (east Scotland)
- Monach Islands SAC (Outer Hebrides)
- North Rona SAC (north west Scotland)

[17] https://sac.jncc.gov.uk/species/S1364/.

- Pembrokeshire Marine SAC (Wales)
- Treshnish Isles (south west Scotland)

In addition, at the following sites, grey seals are a qualifying interest feature, but not a primary reason for site selection:

- Cardigan Bay SAC (Wales)
- Humber Estuary SAC (east England)
- Isles of Scilly Complex SAC (Cornwall)
- Lundy SAC (west England)
- Pen Llyn a'r Sarnau SAC (Wales)
- The Maidens SAC (Northern Ireland)

Ramsar sites

Cetaceans and pinnipeds are not directly protected as species under the Ramsar Convention on Wetlands of International Importance, as the Convention itself is primarily focussed on the conservation and use of wetlands and their ecological character, rather than on specific animal species. However, the Ramsar Convention does require protection of the ecological character of listed wetlands, which may provide important habitats for some species and populations of marine mammals, meaning that these species and populations might benefit indirectly from Ramsar site designation and management.

Seals as notified features of Sites of Special Scientific Interest in England

SSSIs can play an important role in the protection of seals and their habitats in certain parts of England and Wales. While this is primarily a terrestrial regime, it can also extend to intertidal and some subtidal areas, including haul-out and breeding sites for seals.

Under section 28(1) WCA 1981, Natural England must notify areas of land which it considers to be "*of special interest by reason of any of its flora, fauna or geological or physiogeographical features*". When notifying a site, Natural England must notify the local planning authority, every owner and occupier of the land and the Secretary of State.[18]

Natural England's notification must specify:

> *"(a) the flora, fauna, or geological or physiogeographical features by reason of which the land is of special interest, and*
>
> *(b) any operations appearing to Natural England to be likely to damage that flora or fauna or those features,*
>
> *and shall contain a statement of Natural England's views about the management of the land (including any views that Natural England may have about the conservation and enhancement of that flora or fauna or those features."*[19]

Such a notification will be set out in a citation, which will detail the features of interest for which a SSSI has been legally notified, as well as other information about the site. Citations typically describe the location, extent and reasons for notification, but it is not always clear which elements of the citation are the notified features, and care must be taken when interpreting these citations, particularly for older sites, as there is

---

18 WCA 1981, section 28(1).

19 WCA 1981, section 28(4).

no uniform format and the language used can vary in clarity and precision.

The following SSSIs include seals in their citations.

Grey seal:

- Aire Point to Carrick Du SSSI
- Boscastle to Widemouth SSSI
- Farne Islands SSSI
- Godrevy Head to St Agnes SSSI
- Humber Estuary SSSI,
- Lundy SSSI
- Norrard Rocks SSSI
- Western Rocks SSSI

Harbour seal:

- Teesmouth and Cleveland Coast SSSI
- The Wash SSSI

These examples demonstrate that the SSSI framework, although primarily terrestrial in scope, can contribute to the protection of important seal habitats in England. However, identifying where and how seals are protected under this regime requires careful interpretation of the SSSI citations, supported – but not determined – by Natural England's views and online tools.

The 'features of interest' for which a SSSI is considered special and has been legally notified, is set out in the citation for that SSSI. Each citation shows details of the SSSI location, size and the date of notification. It also describes the reasons for notification and the special habitats, geology, plants and / or animals that are found at the site. In addition to the SSSI citation, Natural England's Designated Sites Viewer[20] online tool is helpful in seeing what, in Natural England's view, the notified special interest features of a site are. However, the SSSI legislation has been evolving since the 1940s, leading to a mixed picture across the series of SSSIs in terms of the quality of their citations. There was not, across that period, one agreed standard format for the writing of SSSI citations. This means that the more recent citations (late 1990s onwards) tend to be easier and clearer to interpret than the older (pre 1990s) citations. As a result, the task of identifying special interest features is not straightforward, especially given that SSSI citations frequently contain descriptions of valuable, but not necessarily special, interest features present on the site.

Furthermore, whilst Natural England's views on what is / is not notified on a SSSI are important and carry weight, one cannot simply rely on Natural England's interpretation alone being correct. This includes the list of features on the Designated Sites Viewer (which is based on Natural England's interpretation of SSSI citations). This issue came to light in the 2019 High Court case of *Langton,*[21] which was a challenge to Natural England's decision-making with regards the SSSI assessments connected with the licences it issued to cull badgers in accordance with the Government's bovine tuberculosis strategy. The judge in *Langton* made the following conclusions:[22]

---

20 https://designatedsites.naturalengland.org.uk/SiteSearch.aspx

21 *R (on the application of Langton) v Secretary of State for Environment, Food and Rural Affairs* [2019] EWHC 597 (Admin).

22 Paragraph H4 of [2020] Env.L.R.1.

1. Fauna or flora mentioned under the *general description* heading would generally *not* be features of special interest.

2. In modern SSSI citations there is a statement giving the "Reasons for Notification" before a "General Description" of the site. The features listed under the "Reasons for Notification" would generally be the features of special interest notified under the statutory provisions and fauna or flora mentioned under the "General Description" would generally not be features of special interest.

3. Older citations were more difficult as they sometimes contained a paragraph at the outset that obviously summarised the features of special interest but often had a single heading dealing with the "Reasons for Notification" and a "General Description" in one paragraph.

4. In identifying the special features in a citation, extraneous materials such as Natural England's list of operations likely to damage the site and its views about management of the site could not assist as their scope was too broad, nor could Natural England's guidelines for the selection of SSSIs provide assistance.

Where seals are notified features of SSSIs, a number of legal protections apply that help safeguard them and their habitats from damaging activities.

Under section 28E WCA 1981, landowners or occupiers of SSSI land are prohibited from carrying out any operation that is likely to damage a notified special interest feature of a SSSI unless they first obtain consent from Natural England. Natural England may grant consent subject to conditions, which must be followed. Failure to seek consent, or to comply with any conditions imposed, is an offence. Importantly, landowners must also ensure that any contractors or third parties acting on their behalf do not carry out damaging operations without consent.

In addition to private landowners, public authorities – referred to as 'section 28G authorities' (such as government departments or local authorities) – are subject to specific duties under sections 28H and 28I WCA 1981. These authorities must take reasonable steps, consistent with the proper exercise of the authority's functions, to further the conservation and enhancement of the special interest features of a SSSI,[23] and must give notice to Natural England before carrying out, in the exercise of their functions, operations likely to damage any of the notified special interest features of the SSSI – referred to as seeking *assent* from Natural England.[24] Accordingly, section 28G authorities must determine whether to notify Natural England based on two key considerations: firstly, on the identification of the notified features of the SSSI; and secondly, on the likelihood of damage resulting from the operation. Under section 28I WCA 1981, section 28G authorities must also notify Natural England before giving permission to a third party to carry out an operation that is likely to damage any of the notified special interest features of a SSSI.

A suite of offences related to the disturbance or damage of notified special interest features of a SSSI are set out in section 28P WCA 1981. These provisions are nuanced and fact-specific, requiring careful legal and ecological assessment to determine whether an offence has been committed. In brief, it is an offence under sections 28P(1), (2), (3), (4), (5), (5A) and (5B) WCA 1981 to carry out an operation likely to damage a notified special interest feature without first notifying Natural England.

Further, the offences under sections 28P(6) and 28P(6A) WCA 1981 both concern the intentional or reckless destruction, damage or disturbance of the notified special interest features. However, the key

23 Section 28G(2) WCA 1981.

24 Section 28H(1) WCA 1981.

distinction between these two offences lies in the knowledge requirement.[25]

Section 28P(6) WCA 1981 creates an offence where a person intentionally or recklessly destroys, damages or disturbs notified special interest features of the SSSI and *knew* that the feature was within a SSSI. In other words, the prosecution must prove that the person was aware they were acting within a designated SSSI.

Section 28P(6A), inserted by section 55(3) of the Natural Environment and Rural Communities Act 2006 (**NERC Act 2006**), creates a similar offence but does not require the defendant to have known that the feature they destroyed, damaged or disturbed was located within a SSSI. The offence still requires intentional or reckless conduct and applies even where the person did not know they were within a SSSI, provided they had no reasonable excuse.

The explanatory memorandum to the NERC Act 2006 clarifies that the purpose of this additional offence was to close a loophole in enforcement, where individuals could escape liability under section 28P(6) WCA 1981 by claiming ignorance of SSSI boundaries. Because of the absence of the knowledge requirement in section 28P(6A) WCA 1981, the offence carries a lesser penalty than under section 28P(6) WCA 1981.

The terms 'destroy', 'damage' and 'disturb' are not defined in the WCA 1981 for the purposes of SSSI protection. Their meaning will vary depending on the nature of the operation and the attributes or sensitivity

25 Section 28P(6A) WCA 1981 was inserted by section 55(3) of the Natural Environment and Rural Communities Act 2006, the Explanatory Memorandum for which states that section 28P(6A) WCA 1981 provides a new offence of intentionally or recklessly destroying or damaging the listed features of a SSSI or disturbing its listed fauna, without reasonable excuse, and that this offence is in addition to that in section 28P(6). The difference between them is that commission of this new offence does not require knowledge that what was destroyed, damaged or disturbed was within an SSSI. Accordingly, it carries a lesser penalty.

of the particular feature. For example, for the Farne Islands SSSI, which includes grey seals within its citation, the list of operations requiring Natural England's consent includes the "*use of vehicles or craft likely to damage surface features or vegetation or disturb breeding seabirds or seals*" and "*recreational or other activities likely to damage surface features or vegetation or disturb breeding seabirds or seals*".

Determining whether an operation requires consent, or whether an offence has occurred, involves expert ecological judgment. This judgment should consider both the nature of the activity and the vulnerability of the feature. While SSSI case law and guidance do not define 'destroy', 'damage' or 'disturbance', useful reference can be made to the European Commission's guidance document on the management of Natura 2000 sites (please see Chapter 6 which discusses this guidance in the context of disturbance). Although the legal thresholds under SSSI law are different from those under the various Habitats Regulations, this framework provides a useful structure for informed thinking about what may constitute 'damage' or 'disturbance' in relation to seal populations protected under domestic conservation designations.

Sites notified as Sites of Special Scientific Interest in Scotland

In Scotland the SSSI regime is dealt with under the Nature Conservation (Scotland) Act 2004[26] and is under the remit of NatureScot.

SSSIs in Scotland that list seals as a notified natural feature include:

Grey seal:

- Oronsay and South Colonsay SSSI

---

[26] Sections 3 – 22 of the Nature Conservation (Scotland) Act 2004 set out the regime for notifying SSSIs, exercising functions in relation to SSSIs and offences and byelaws.

- Small Seal Islands SSSI
- Faray and Holm of Faray SSSI
- Isle of May SSSI
- Treshnish Isles SSSI
- North Rona and Sula Sgeir SSSI
- Muckle and Little Green Holm SSSI
- North Fetlar SSSI

Harbour seal:

- East Sanday Coast SSSI
- Eynhallow SSSI
- Mousa SSSI
- North Fetlar SSSI
- Tayport – Tentsmuir Coast SSSI

Under section 19(1) of the Nature Conservation (Scotland) Act 2004, any person who intentionally or recklessly damages any natural feature specified in a SSSI notification is, subject to an incidental result defence set out in section 19(2), guilty of an offence. Further, section 58(3) states that a protected natural feature consisting of fauna, is for the purposes of the Nature Conservation (Scotland) Act 2004, to be treated as being damaged if it is disturbed or harassed to the extent that NatureScot (a) no longer consider the land to which it relates to be of special interest by reason of that feature, or (b) consider the degree to which the land is of special interest by reason of that feature to have decreased significantly.

Nature Conservation Marine Protected Areas

Nature Conservation Marine Protected Areas (**NCMPAs**) are another legal mechanism for site-based marine conservation in Scotland. They were introduced by the Marine (Scotland) Act 2010 for the inshore region (0-12nm).

Under section 67(1) of the Marine (Scotland) Act 2010, Scottish Ministers may, by a 'designation order', designate an area as a NCMPA. Before designating an area as a NCMPA, the Scottish Ministers must have regard to the extent to which the designation of the area would contribute towards the development of a network of conservation sites.[27] The designation order must identify the site boundaries[28] and the protected features and set out the conservation objectives for those features.[29]

Public authorities are under a statutory duty to exercise their functions in a manner which furthers – or, if that is not possible, least hinders – the conservation objectives of NCMPAs.[30]

The Scottish Ministers may make a marine conservation order in order to further the stated conservation objectives of an NCMPA, for example, to impose restrictions or prohibitions on certain activities.[31]

---

27 Marine (Scotland) Act 2010, section 68(4).

28 Marine (Scotland) Act 2010, section 69(1).

29 Marine (Scotland) Act 2010, section 68(3).

30 Marine (Scotland) Act 2010, section 82(2).

31 Marine (Scotland) Act 2010, sections 85-91.

While many NCMPAs in Scotland are designated for benthic habitats, three sites are specifically designated for cetaceans. These are:

- North East Lewis NCMPA, which includes the Risso's dolphin as a protected feature;
- The Sea of the Hebrides NCMPA, which includes the minke whale as a protected feature; and
- The Southern Trench NCMPA, which includes the minke whale as a protected feature.

Marine Conservation Zones

In the English and Welsh inshore region (0-12nm) and the offshore region of the UK (12-200nm), under section 116 of the Marine and Coastal Access Act 2009, the appropriate authority may designate Marine Conservation Zones (**MCZs**) for the purpose of conserving marine flora or fauna, marine habitats or types of marine habitat or features of geological or geomorphological interest.[32] Designation orders must set out the protected features and conservation objectives for the MCZ.[33] Public authorities exercising functions that could affect the protected features of an MCZ or any ecological or geomorphological process on which the conservation of any protected feature of an MCZ is (wholly or in part) dependent, must (so far as is consistent with their proper exercise), exercise its functions in the manner which the authority considers best furthers the conservation objectives for the MCZ, or where this is not possible, at least not hinder them.[34] The MMO has the power to make byelaws for the purpose of furthering the conservation objectives

32 Marine and Coastal Access Act 2009, section 117(1).

33 Marine and Coastal Access Act 2009, section 117(2).

34 Marine and Coastal Access Act 2009, section 125.

stated for an MCZ in England[35] or in relation to the exploitation of sea fisheries resources in England for the purposes of conserving marine fauna in England and the English offshore region.[36] Similar provisions exist for the inshore and offshore regions of Wales, Scotland and Northern Ireland.[37]

To date, no MCZs have been designated with marine mammals as a protected feature. Efforts to designate an MCZ in Lyme Bay, an area identified as being important for white-beaked dolphins, were not taken forward.

At present, Scotland's three NCMPAs for cetaceans – two for minke whale and one for Risso's dolphin – remain the only examples of site-based protection in the UK specifically for cetacean species that are not listed as Annex II species under the Habitats Directive. Their rarity highlights the inherent difficulty of designating MPAs for wide-ranging cetaceans that fall outside existing European site frameworks. Challenges include the mobility of these species, which makes it harder to identify discrete, evidence-based areas of critical importance, and the policy and political reluctance to impose spatial restrictions without the clear legal driver that Annex II listing provides. As a result, while the legislative tools exist, their use for non-Annex II cetaceans has so far been exceptional rather than routine.

MANAGEMENT OF SACs

Once a site has been designated as an SAC and has become part of the National Site Network, the various Habitats Regulations impose specific obligations on the appropriate authority to manage, and where necessary

35 Marine and Coastal Access Act 2009, section 129.

36 Marine and Coastal Access Act 2009, sections 129A and 129B.

37 Marine and Coastal Access Act 2009, sections 134, 134A, 134B, 134C, 137A, 137E.

adapt, the National Site Network, with a view to contributing to the achievement of the management objectives of the National Site Network for that site with a view to attaining the sites conservation objectives.

The various Habitats Regulations all contain the following wording which sets out the management objectives of the national site network, as appropriate to Annex II marine mammal SACs:

> *"to maintain at, or where appropriate, restore to, a favourable conservation status in their natural range (so far as it lies in the United Kingdom's territory, and so far as is proportionate) [...] the species listed in Annex II to the Habitats Directive whose natural range includes any part of the UK's territory"*[38]

The term '*favourable conservation status*', is defined by reference to Article 1(i) of the Habitats Directive, which provides that:

> *"conservation status of a species means the sum of the influences acting on the species concerned that may affect the long-term distribution and abundance of its populations within the territory referred to in Article 2;*
>
> *The conservation status of a species will be taken as 'favourable' when:*
>
> - *population dynamics data on the species concerned indicate that it is maintaining itself on a long-term basis as a viable component of its natural habitats, and;*

[38] Conservation of Habitats and Species Regulations 2017, regulation 16A(a)(ii); Conservation (Natural Habitats, &c.) Regulations 1994, regulation 9D(2)(a)(ii); Conservation of Offshore Marine Habitats and Species Regulations 2017, regulation 18A(2)(a)(ii); The Conservation (Natural Habitats, etc.) Regulations (Northern Ireland) 1995 (as amended), regulation 8C.

- *the natural range of the species is neither being reduced nor is likely to be reduced for the foreseeable future, and;*

- *there is, and will probably continue to be, a sufficiently large habitat to maintain its populations on a long-term basis."*

This definition underscores the importance of managing marine sites not only to prevent harm but also to support the long-term viability of marine mammal populations.

In addition to active management, the condition of sites forming part of the National Site Network – as well as SSSIs – is monitored through the Common Standards Monitoring approach.[39] This monitoring framework assesses whether conservation objectives are being achieved, classifying sites as being in "*favourable*", "*unfavourable-recovering*", "*unfavourable*" or "*destroyed (in whole or part)*" condition. For marine mammal features, monitoring may include data on population size, reproductive success, habitat quality and levels of human disturbance.

Designation also gives rise to regulatory powers. For example, under the Conservation of Habitats and Species Regulations 2017, the appropriate authority may issue a "special nature conservation order" which specifies operations which could destroy or damage protected features under certain circumstances and serve "stop notices" in relation to operations that could damage designated features of the site.[40] Although, to date, stop notices have never been used by Ministers, this provision provides an important tool to prevent or halt harmful activities that threaten marine mammal habitats.

[39] https://jncc.gov.uk/our-work/common-standards-monitoring/

[40] Conservation of Habitats and Species Regulations 2017, regulations 27 and 28.

Moreover, the various Habitats Regulations enable the creation of byelaws for management activities within designated sites,[41] though none have been designated for marine mammals to date.

SUMMARY

The designation of SACs for marine mammals under the Habitats Directive – now assimilated into UK law – has played a pivotal role in recognising the ecological significance of key habitats for harbour porpoise, bottlenose dolphin, grey and harbour seals. Despite the complexities of identifying fixed sites for highly mobile species, legal action and sustained scientific advocacy have resulted in a substantial network of protected areas. However, site designation alone does not ensure effective conservation. Legal duties continue beyond the point of designation, requiring that plans or projects which are likely to have a significant effect on these sites must undergo a rigorous process of assessment and decision-making. The next chapter explores this in detail, examining how the Habitats Regulations Assessment operates to safeguard marine mammals within and associated with protected sites.

41 Conservation of Habitats and Species Regulations 2017, regulation 32; Conservation (Natural Habitats, &c.) Regulations 1994, regulations 28-31.

CHAPTER THREE

THE HABITATS REGULATIONS ASSESSMENT PROCESS AND MARINE MAMMALS

INTRODUCTION

Once marine mammal SACs have been designated, ongoing legal protection is primarily delivered through the Habitats Regulations Assessment (**HRA**) process (Habitats Regulations Appraisal in Scotland). Under the various Habitats Regulations in the UK's devolved jurisdictions, any plan or project likely to have a significant effect on a European site – including marine SACs – must undergo HRA. This assessment ensures that such plans or projects do not adversely affect the integrity of the site by undermining the conservation objectives of its protected features, including marine mammals.

HRA plays a central role in safeguarding SACs for marine mammals from human activities. The process is legally stringent and precautionary, requiring detailed ecological data and mitigation measures to avoid or reduce potential impacts.

This chapter explores the HRA regime as it applies to marine mammals, setting out the legal requirements and stages of the assessment process.

ARTICLE 6 OF THE HABITATS DIRECTIVE

The HRA process originates from the EU Habitats Directive and is embedded in UK law through the various Habitats Regulations. It applies to any plan or project that is likely to have a significant effect on an SAC, either alone or in combination with other plans or projects. The legal framework for HRA is set out in Articles 6(3) and (4) of the Habitats Directive, which establish a stepwise approach for assessing and mitigating potential impacts on the integrity of SACs.[1]

Article 6(3) of the Habitats Directive states:

> *"Any plan or project not directly connected with or necessary to the management of the site but likely to have a significant effect thereon, either individually or in combination with other plans or projects, shall be subject to appropriate assessment of its implications for the site in view of the site's conservation objectives. In the light of the conclusions of the assessment of the implications for the site and subject to the provisions of paragraph 4, the competent national authorities shall agree to the plan or project only after having ascertained that it will not adversely affect the integrity of the site concerned and, if appropriate, after having obtained the opinion of the general public."*

Article 6(4) states:

> *"If, in spite of a negative assessment of the implications for the site and in the absence of alternative solutions, a plan or project must nevertheless be carried out for imperative reasons of overriding public interest, including those of a social or economic nature, the Member States shall take all compensatory measures necessary to ensure that the overall coherence of Natura 2000 is protected. It shall inform the Commission of the compensatory measures adopted.*
>
> *Where the site concerned hosts a priority natural habitat type and / or a priority species, the only considerations which may be raised are those relating to human health or public safety, to beneficial consequences of primary importance for the environment or, further to an opinion of*

[1] Please note however, that the analysis of compliance with Article 6 starts with Article 6(1) and 6(2) to enhance sites and prevent harm. This is beyond the scope of this book.

the Commission, to other imperative reasons of overriding public interest."

Implementation of Article 6 into UK law

Part 6 of The Conservation of Habitats and Species Regulations 2017[2] transposes the Article 6(3) language and provides a framework for decision making when a plan or project is proposed that has the potential to impact on the sites or their features.

Regulation 63 states:

"Assessment of implications for European sites and European offshore marine sites

63.

(1) A competent authority, before deciding to undertake, or give any consent, permission or other authorisation for, a plan or project which –

(a) is likely to have a significant effect on a European site or a European offshore marine site (either alone or in combination with other plans or projects), and

(b) is not directly connected with or necessary to the management of that site,

2 Regulations 48 to 53 of the Conservation (Natural Habitats, &c.) Regulations 1994; regulations 43 – 48 of the Conservation (Natural Habitats, etc.) Regulations (Northern Ireland) 1995; and regulations 28-36 of the Conservation of Offshore Marine Habitats and Species Regulations 2017 provide the HRA framework in their respective jurisdictions.

must make an appropriate assessment of the implications of the plan or project for that site in view of that site's conservation objectives.

(2) A person applying for any such consent, permission or other authorisation must provide such information as the competent authority may reasonably require for the purposes of the assessment or to enable it to determine whether an appropriate assessment is required.

(3) The competent authority must for the purposes of the assessment consult the appropriate nature conservation body and have regard to any representations made by that body within such reasonable time as the authority specifies.

(4) It must also, if it considers it appropriate, take the opinion of the general public, and if it does so, it must take such steps for that purpose as it considers appropriate.

(5) In the light of the conclusions of the assessment, and subject to regulation 64, the competent authority may agree to the plan or project only after having ascertained that it will not adversely affect the integrity of the European site or the European offshore marine site (as the case may be).

(6) In considering whether a plan or project will adversely affect the integrity of the site, the competent authority must have regard to the manner in which it is proposed to be carried out or to any conditions or restrictions subject to which it proposes that the consent, permission or other authorisation should be given.

…"

Regulation 64 of the Conservation of Habitats and Species Regulations 2017 transposes Article 6(4) of the Habitats Directive as follows:

"Consideration of overriding public interest

64.

(1) If the competent authority is satisfied that, there being no alternative solutions, the plan or project must be carried out for imperative reasons of overriding public interest (which, subject to paragraph (2), may be of a social or economic nature), it may agree to the plan or project notwithstanding a negative assessment of the implications for the European site or the European offshore marine site (as the case may be).

(2) Where the site concerned hosts a priority natural habitat type or a priority species, the reasons referred to in paragraph (1) must be either –

(a) reasons relating to human health, public safety or beneficial consequences of primary importance to the environment; or

(b) any other reasons which the competent authority, having due regard to the opinion of the appropriate authority, considers to be imperative reasons of overriding public interest."

Regulation 68 of the Conservation of Habitats and Species Regulations 2017 transposes the remainder of Article 6(4) insofar as it relates to compensatory measures as follows:

"Compensatory measures

68. When in accordance with regulation 64 – (a) a plan or project is agreed to, notwithstanding a negative assessment of the implications for a European site or a European offshore marine site, or (b) a decision, or a consent, permission or other authorisation, is affirmed on review, notwithstanding such an assessment, the appropriate authority must secure that any necessary compensatory measures are taken to ensure that the overall coherence of Natura 2000 is protected."

A 'plan or project'

A 'plan or project' is not defined within the Habitats Directive, nor any of the various Habitats Regulations. There is though, a body of case law that says that the words are to be given a wide meaning. Accordingly, development of offshore infrastructure will, in nearly all circumstances, constitute a plan or project.

The 2018 EU Guidance on *Managing Natura 2000*[3] (**Natura 2000 Guidance**) provides further detail on interpreting[4] what constitutes a 'plan or project' and why it should be given a broad interpretation. The Natura 2000 Guidance advises, in considering such interpretation, that the Habitats Directive does not circumscribe the scope of either 'plan' or 'project' by reference to particular categories of either, instead, the key limiting factor is whether or not they are likely to have a significant effect on a site.[5] This was also the position taken in domestic case law by Owen J in *Akester*.[6]

---

3 EU Guidance, *Managing Natura 2000,* Commission Notice C(2018) 7621 final, Brussels, 21.11.2018.

4 While EU guidance documents are not legally binding, they may continue to be used to inform the interpretation and application of assimilated EU law in the UK following Brexit. Under the European Union (Withdrawal) Act 2018, assimilated EU law is to be interpreted in line with assimilated EU case law and principles (section 6). Although the Retained EU Law (Revocation and Reform) Act 2023 repealed some elements of assimilated EU law, it did not prevent the continued use of EU guidance documents where they provide helpful context to the interpretation of UK law that originated from EU law (such as the various Habitats Regulations). As such, EU guidance remains a relevant interpretative aid.

5 EU Guidance, *Managing Natura 2000*, paragraph 4.4.

6 *R (Akester) v Department for Environment, Food and Rural Affairs and another* [2010] EWHC 232 (Admin).

The Natura 2000 Guidance goes on to advise that support for a broad definition of 'project' is reinforced, by analogy, by referring to Directive 2011/92/EU *on the assessment of the effects of certain public and private projects on the environment* (as amended by Directive 2014/52/EU) (**the EIA Directive**). Article 1(2)(a) of the EIA Directive provides that 'project' means:

> *" – the execution of construction works or of other installations or schemes,*
>
> *– other interventions in the natural surroundings and landscape including those involving the extraction of mineral resources."*

The Natura 2000 Guidance clarifies that this broad definition extends beyond physical construction and includes other interventions in the natural environment, such as regular activities that utilise natural resources. For instance, a significant intensification of agriculture that damages or destroys the semi-natural character of a site may be covered.

In addition, the CJEU has issued a number of rulings regarding the type of interventions which require the application of Article 6(3).

The *Waddenzee*[7] case, which related to authorisations granted for cockle fishing in the Netherlands Wadden Sea, clarified that activities which have been carried out periodically for several years on the site concerned but for which a licence is granted annually for a limited period, with each licence entailing a new assessment both of the possibility of carrying on that activity and of the site where it may be carried on, should be considered, at the time of each application, as a distinct plan or project within the meaning of Article 6(3).

---

7 Landelijke Vereniging tot Behoud van de Waddenzee v Staatssecretaris van Landbouw (Cooperatieve Producentenorganisatie van de Nederlandse Kokkelvisserij UA, intervening) C-127/02, paragraphs 25-29.

In the *Papenburg* case[8] the CJEU further ruled that: "*...ongoing maintenance works in respect of the navigable channels of estuaries, which are not concerned with or necessary to the management of the site... must, to the extent that they constitute a project and are likely to have a significant effect on the site concerned, undergo an assessment of their implications for that site pursuant to those provisions [Article 6(3)]*".

However, "*...if, having regard in particular to the regularity or nature of the maintenance works at issue... or the conditions under which they are carried out, they can be regarded as constituting a single operation, in particular where they are designed to maintain the navigable channel at a certain depth by means of regular dredging necessary for that purpose, those maintenance works can be considered to be one and the same project for the purposes of Article 6(3) of the Habitats Directive.*"

The Dutch Nitrogen case[9] builds upon the reasoning in *Papenburg*, offering further clarity on how recurring or cyclical activities may still constitute a "project" for the purposes of Article 6(3). In particular, the CJEU confirmed that the application of fertilisers by farmers constituted a "project", notwithstanding its recurring nature. The activity was considered a "single operation" due to its common objective – namely, crop cultivation – its consistency in location and its regularity over time. However, the CJEU also introduced an important temporal qualification: where such an activity was lawfully authorised and continuously practiced prior to Article 6(3) becoming applicable to the Natura 2000 site, it may fall outside the scope of the assessment obligation. This exemption does not apply where there has been a break in continuity or a change in location or conditions – such circumstances

---

8 *Stadt Papenburg v Bundesrepublik Deutschland*, C-226/08, paragraphs 50-51.

9 *Joined Cases C-293/17 and C-294/17 Coöperatie Mobilisation for the Environment and Vereniging Leefmilieu v College van gedeputeerde staten van Limburg and College van gedeputeerde staten van Gelderland* (Dutch Nitrogen Case)

would render the activity a "new project" for which an appropriate assessment under Article 6(3) would be required.

The Natura 2000 Guidance also discusses what a 'plan' is, advising that the term 'plan' has also, for the purposes of Article 6(3), a potentially very broad meaning and refers, by analogy, to Directive 2001/42/EC *on the assessment of the effects of certain plans and programmes on the environment* (**SEA Directive**). Article 2(a) of the SEA Directive defines plans and programmes as:

> *"Plans and programmes, including those co-financed by the European Community, as well as any modifications to them:*
>
> - *which are subject to preparation and/or adoption by an authority at national, regional or local level or which are prepared by an authority for adoption, through a legislative procedure by Parliament or Government, and*
>
> - *which are required by legislative, regulatory or administrative provisions."*

In summary, in the marine environment, the concept of a "plan or project" under Article 6(3) should be interpreted broadly. It is well established that this includes a wide range of activities, particularly those involving infrastructure development, where such activities are likely to have a significant effect on a designated site. This would encompass proposals such as offshore renewable energy infrastructure, port developments, subsea cables and dredging.

The principles emerging from *Papenburg* and the *Dutch Nitrogen* case also suggest that fishing operations may, depending on their nature and context, constitute a "plan or project" under Article 6(3). While some forms of fishing – particularly those that are authorised, recurring and consistently undertaken in the same area – may potentially fall outside the scope of Article 6(3) where continuity is established, changes in location, method, intensity or the target species could trigger the requirement for an HRA. Ultimately, whether fishing constitutes a "plan or project" must be determined on a case-by-case basis, taking into account the specific characteristics of the activity and its potential to affect the Conservation Objectives of nearby Natura 2000 / National Site Network sites.

THE HRA PROCESS IN RELATION TO MARINE MAMMALS

The HRA process follows a stepwise approach, and the assessment and derogations must be carried out in that order. Firstly, the Appropriate Assessment – if adverse effects on integrity cannot be ruled out, then derogation tests must be met. There must be no alternative solutions and imperative reasons of overriding public interest. If the plan or project is then to be agreed, the appropriate authority must secure that any necessary compensatory measures are taken to ensure the overall coherence of the National Site Network is protected. These steps are set out below.

'Screening' of a Plan or Project – when is an 'Appropriate Assessment' required?

The first step under the HRA process is to determine whether a plan or project is *"likely to have a significant effect"* on an SAC.

Where a competent authority is considering whether to undertake, or authorise, a plan or project that is not directly connected with or necessary to the management of the site, it must assess, on the basis of objective information, whether significant effects on the site can be ruled out. If not, an Appropriate Assessment is required. This principle was established in *Waddenzee*, where the CJEU held that:

> *"...Article 6(3) of the Habitats Directive must be interpreted as meaning that any plan or project not directly connected with or necessary to the management of the site is to be subject to an appropriate assessment of its implications for the site in view of the site's*

conservation objectives if it cannot be excluded, on the basis of objective information, that it will have a significant effect on that site, either individually or in combination with other plans or projects."[10]

This question of whether likely significant effects can be excluded at the outset is often referred to as the 'screening' test.

The UK Supreme Court considered this process in *R (Champion) v North Norfolk District Council,*[11] a case involving both EIA and HRA, and emphasised the simplicity of the threshold:

> *"The process envisaged by art 6(3) should not be over-complicated.... in cases where it is not obvious, the competent authority will consider whether the "trigger" for appropriate assessment is met (and see paras 41-43 of Waddenzee). But this informal threshold decision is not to be confused with a formal "screening opinion" in the EIA sense. The operative words are those of the Habitats Directive itself. All that is required is that, in a case where the authority has found there to be a risk of significant adverse effects to a protected site, there should be an "appropriate assessment"."*

Thus, while the term 'screening' is used in HRA, it does not equate to the formal screening stage found in EIA processes. Under HRA, the legal requirement is clear: the competent authority must consider whether the plan or project, alone or in combination with others, may have a significant effect on the site's conservation objectives. If such an effect cannot be ruled out, an appropriate assessment must follow.

Importantly, a precautionary approach must be taken. In *Waddenzee*, the CJEU made clear that the threshold is a low one, stating that a plan or project must undergo appropriate assessment *"if it cannot be excluded, on the basis of objective information that the plan or project will have significant*

10 *Waddenzee*, C-127/02, paragraph 45.

11 *R (on the application of Champion) v North Norfolk District Council and another* [2015] 4 All ER 169, para 41.

effects on the site concerned".[12] This was reinforced in *Sweetman v An Bord Pleanala,*[13] where Advocate General Sharpston described the threshold at the first stage of Article 6(3) as *"a very low one"*.

In *R (Wyatt) v Fareham Borough Council),*[14] the Court of Appeal held that Article 6(3) "*embodies the "precautionary principle" and makes it possible effectively to prevent adverse effects on the integrity of protected sites as a result of the plans or projects being considered.*"

Appropriate Assessment

Once it is determined that a plan or project is likely to have a significant effect on a protected site, an Appropriate Assessment is required under Article 6(3).

There is a substantial body of case law interpreting Article 6(3) of the Habitats Directive and regulation 63 of the Conservation of Habitats and Species Regulations 2017, stemming both from the CJEU and the domestic courts. Some key principles have become well-established. These are summarised nicely in the Court of Appeal judgment in *Wyatt,*[15] and are discussed below:

The role of expert advice

A competent authority is entitled, and can be expected, to give significant weight to the advice of expert statutory bodies, such as Natural England. This principle is supported by case law including *Smyth*[16] and *Preston v*

---

12 *Waddenzee,* paragraph 44.

13 *Sweetman v An Bord Pleanala*, C-258/11, paragraph 49.

14 *R (on the application of Wyatt) v Fareham BC* [2022] EWCA Civ 983, paragraph 6.

15 Ibid, paragraph 9.

16 *Smyth v Secretary of State for Communities and Local Government* [2015] EWCA Civ 174, paragraph 84.

Cumbria County Council.[17] An authority is not bound to follow such advice, but where it chooses to depart from it, cogent reasons must be provided. This requirement was highlighted by Baroness Hale in *Morge v Hampshire County Council*[18] and reaffirmed in *Prideaux v Buckinghamshire County Council.*[19] Courts will in turn afford a level of deference to expert regulatory bodies, especially where decisions involve complex scientific or technical matters. This is illustrated in *Mott v Environment Agency*[20] and echoed in numerous judgments.

The precautionary principle and the standard of certainty

The requirement in the second sentence of Article 6(3) of the Habitats Directive and in regulation 63(5) embodies the "*precautionary principle, and makes it possible effectively to prevent adverse effects on the integrity of protected sites as result of the plans or projects being considered*".[21] As established in *Waddenzee*, this principle requires a high standard of investigation[22] and the duty placed on the competent authority is to ascertain that there will be no adverse effects on the integrity of the protected site. Importantly, however, this certainty is not synonymous with "absolute certainty". Rather, the competent authority must be "*satisfied that there is no reasonable doubt as to the absence of adverse effects*

---

17 *R(on the application of Preston) v Cumbria County Council* [2019] EWHC 1362 (Admin), paragraph 69.

18 *R(on the application of Morge) v Hampshire County Council* [2011] 1WLR 268, paragraph 45.

19 *R(on the application of Prideux) v Buckinghamshire County Council* [2013] Env LR 32, paragraph 116.

20 *R(on the application of Mott) v Environment Agency* [2016] 1 WLR 4338, paragraphs 69 – 77.

21 *Waddenzee,* paragraph 58.

22 *Waddenzee,* paragraphs 44, 58, 59 and 61.

on the integrity of the site concerned".[23] In *Waddenzee*, at paragraph 59, the CJEU emphasised the responsibility of the competent authority, having taken account of the conclusions of the appropriate assessment, to authorise the proposed development *"only if [it] has made certain that it will not adversely affect the integrity of that site"*. That, it said, *"is the case where no reasonable scientific doubt remains as to the absence of such effects"*. But, as Advocate General Kokott explained in *Wadenzee* (in paragraphs 102 to 106 of her opinion), a requirement of "absolute certainty" would be "disproportionate". As she said (at paragraph 107), "*the necessary certainty cannot be construed as meaning absolute certainty...*", the conclusion of an appropriate assessment is, *"of necessity, subjective in nature"*, and "*competent authorities can, from their point of view, be certain that there will be no adverse effects even though, from an objective point of view, there is no absolute certainty"*. Similar observations appear in the judgment itself (in paragraphs 44, 58, 59 and 61). As the Supreme Court acknowledged in *Champion*,[24] adopting the approach in *Waddenzee*, *"while a high standard of investigation is demanded, the issue ultimately rests on the judgment of the authority"*. This approach is, in essence, what the "precautionary principle" requires in the context of Article 6(3) of the Habitats Directive and regulation 63 of the Habitats Regulations.

Reasonable doubt and worst-case scenarios

The requirement that there be *"no reasonable doubt as to the absence of adverse effects on the integrity of the site concerned"* does not mean that the *"reasonable worst-case scenario"* must always be assessed. In the European Commission guidance document, *Communication on the precautionary*

---

[23] *Waddenzee*, paragraphs 44, 58, 59 and 61; paragraphs 107 and 108 of the Advocate General's opinion in *Waddenzee*; and *Holohan v An Bord Pleanala* (Case C-461/17), paragraphs 33 – 37.

[24] *R (on the application of Champion) v North Norfolk District Council* [2015] UKSC 52, paragraph 41.

principle,[25] it is stated in Annex III that *"[when] the available data are inadequate or non-conclusive, a prudent and cautious approach to environmental protection, health or safety could be to opt for the worst-case hypothesis"*. That guidance, however, is not law, nor is it in mandatory terms. What is required in law is a sufficient degree of certainty to ensure that there is "no reasonable doubt" on the relevant question. It may sometimes be useful to consider a "reasonable worst-case scenario" when assessing whether the necessary degree of certainty has been achieved. But whether there are grounds for "reasonable doubt" will always be a matter of judgment in the particular case.[26]

Scientific rigour and best available knowledge

An appropriate assessment must be founded on the "*best scientific knowledge in the field*", as held in *Holohan.*[27] Such knowledge must be both up-to-date and not merely an expert's bare assertion.[28] And the concept of "best scientific knowledge" is not a wholly free-standing requirement, separate from the precautionary principle itself. It is inherent in the precautionary principle, and in the concept of "no reasonable doubt".[29]

Content and quality of an appropriate assessment

What is required of the competent authority, therefore, is a case-specific assessment in which the applicable science is brought to bear with sufficient rigour on the implications of the project for the protected site concerned. If an appropriate assessment is to comply with Article 6(3) of

---

25 Commission of the European Communities, *Communication from the Commission on the precautionary principle,* COM(2000) 1 final, Brussels, 2.2.2000.

26 *Wyatt,* paragraph 9.

27 *Holohan*, paragraph 33.

28 *Smyth*, paragraph 83; *Wyatt,* paragraph 9.

29 *Wyatt,* paragraph 9.

the Habitats Directive, it *"cannot have lacunae and must contain complete, precise and definitive findings and conclusions capable of removing all reasonable scientific doubt as to the effects of the proposed works on the protected site concerned".*[30]

The role of the Competent Authority

The obligation under Article 6(3) and regulation 63 (and the equivalent provisions in the various Habitats Regulations) falls on competent authorities, not on the courts. Whether a plan or project is likely to have an adverse effect on the integrity of a European site is a matter of evaluative judgment for the authority itself. This principle was emphasised in *Holohan* and reinforced in domestic jurisprudence including *Champion* and *Smyth.* Courts are not empowered or equipped to carry out the assessment themselves. Instead, their role is a supervisory one, reviewing whether the competent authority has lawfully discharged its duty. This supervisory function has been reiterated consistently in cases such as *Compton Parish Council v Guildford Borough Council.*[31]

The supervisory role of the Courts

While the courts do not undertake an appropriate assessment themselves, the CJEU has recognised in *Dutch Nitrogen* that it is *"for the national courts to carry out a thorough and in-depth examination of the scientific soundness of the "appropriate assessment" ... "*[32] which *"makes it possible to ensure that there is no reasonable scientific doubt as to the absence of adverse effects of each plan or project on the integrity of the site concerned, which it is for the national court to ascertain"*[33] This requirement means the court

30 *Sweetman v An Bord Pleanala* (C-258/11), paragraph 44) and *People Over Wind v Coillte Teoranta* (C-323/17), paragraph 38; *Wyatt,* paragraph 9.

31 *Compton Parish Council v Guildford Borough Council* [2020] JPL 661, paragraph 207.

32 *Dutch Nitrogen,* Case C-293/17, paragraph 101.

33 *Dutch Nitrogen,* C-293/17, paragraph 104.

must be fully satisfied that the authority's approach was lawful and scientifically robust. However, there is nothing in EU case law to suggest that this supervisory function transforms the court into a parallel decision-maker undertaking its own Appropriate Assessment.

Taking account of mitigation measures

The role of mitigation at the screening and appropriate assessment stages was clarified by the CJEU in *Sweetman v An bord Pleanala* (known as *'People Over Wind*)[34]. The case asked:

> *"Whether measures intended to avoid or reduce the harmful effects of a plan or project on the site concerned can be taken into consideration at the screening stage, in order to determine whether it is necessary to carry out an appropriate assessment...?"*

The CJEU ruled that mitigation cannot be considered at the screening stage. Since mitigation is designed to avoid or reduce harmful effects, its use presupposes that there is a risk of such effects occurring. Therefore:

> *"Taking account of such measures at the screening stage would be liable to compromise the practical effect of the Habitats Directive in general, and the assessment stage in particular, as the latter stage would be deprived of its purpose and there would be a risk of circumvention of that stage, which constitutes, however, an essential safeguard provided for by the directive."*[35]

This position differs from that under the EIA regime (see Chapter 4), where certain mitigation measures may be considered at the screening stage, a position that is not impacted by the judgment in *People Over Wind.*

---

[34] *People Over Wind v Coillte Teoranta*, C-323/17, paragraph 31.

[35] *People Over Wind v Coillte Teoranta*, C-323/17, paragraph 37.

The Appropriate Assessment decision

The decision stage is governed by Article 6(3), which provides:

> *"the competent national authorities shall agree to the plan or project only after having ascertained that it will not adversely affect the integrity of the site concerned and, if appropriate, after having obtained the opinion of the general public."*

At this point, the competent authority may consider mitigation measures, but only insofar as they remove any risk of an adverse effect on the integrity of the site. If the assessment concludes that the project will not have an adverse effect, taking mitigation into account where appropriate, consent may be granted.

However, if it cannot be demonstrated with certainty that the plan or project will not adversely affect the integrity of the site, then consent must be refused – unless the applicant can demonstrate that there are no alternative solutions and that the project must proceed for imperative reasons of overriding public interest, in which case the Article 6(4) derogation process must be followed.

Article 6(4) – Alternative Solutions and Imperative Reasons of Overriding Public Interest (IROPI)

Where an appropriate assessment cannot rule out an adverse effect on the integrity of a protected site, Article 6(4) of the Habitats Directive allows a plan or project to proceed only if specific and stringent conditions are met. The first step in this derogation process is to consider whether there are alternative solutions.

Alternative Solutions

The competent authority must first assess whether alternative solutions exist that would meet the objectives of the plan or project while avoiding damage to the protected site. Alternatives must be feasible and capable of delivering the same or similar genuine or critical objectives with less environmental harm.

In assessing alternatives, authorities must examine all reasonable options that could achieve the project's purpose. The test is not whether there is an identical alternative, but whether there are less damaging, feasible ways to meet the relevant objectives.

Priority Habitats or Species

The next consideration is whether the site in question hosts a priority natural habitat type or a priority species. If so, the scope for justifying harm is much narrower. This is reflected, for example, in regulation 64(2) of the Conservation of Habitats and Species Regulations 2017, which states:

> *"Where the site concerned hosts a priority natural habitat type or a priority species, the reasons referred to in paragraph (1) must be either –*
>
> *(a) reasons relating to human health, public safety or beneficial consequences of primary importance to the environment; or*
>
> *(b) any other reasons which the competent authority, having due regard to the opinion of the appropriate authority, considers to be imperative reasons of overriding public interest."*

This requirement reinforces the higher level of protection afforded to priority features and limits the grounds on which derogation can be justified.

Imperative Reasons of Overriding Public Interest (IROPI)

If no alternative solutions exist, the next step is for the competent authority to assess whether IROPI justify proceeding. The concept of IROPI is not defined in the Habitats Directive, however, the Natura

2000 Guidance, advises that the competent authority must be able to demonstrate that:

- the plan or project is imperative, i.e., the plan or project must be required or indispensable;[36]

- have a clear public interest that is overriding – it is therefore clear that not every kind of public interest of a social or economic nature is sufficient[37] and whatever the benefits are, they must be evidenced to demonstrate that they outweigh the potential damage to the site; and

- the interest must be long-term.[38]

Article 6(4) – Compensation

Where a plan or project is permitted to proceed despite a negative appropriate assessment and the absence of alternative solutions – on the basis of IROPI – Article 6(4) of the Habitats Directive requires that the Member State must adopt all necessary compensatory measures to ensure the overall coherence of Natura 2000 (the National Site Network) is protected.

In recent years, the need for such compensatory measures has become increasingly prevalent in the context of offshore wind development, where adverse effects on the integrity of protected sites – particularly for seabird species – cannot be ruled out under the HRA process. This is particularly evident in relation to kittiwake, with artificial nesting

36 EU Guidance, *Managing Natura 2000*, paragraph 5.3.2.

37 Ibid.

38 Ibid.

structures now embedded as compensatory measures in Development Consent Orders for projects such as Hornsea Three and Hornsea Four.[39]

Looking ahead, similar compensation requirements may arise for marine mammals, especially in relation to SACs designated for harbour porpoise, given the spatial scale of these SACs and the acoustic sensitivity and mobile nature of harbour porpoise. Potential compensatory measures for harbour porpoise could include:

- Spatial and temporal restrictions on high-noise activities (e.g., pile driving);
- Investment in bycatch reduction programmes; and
- Funding for broader conservation and monitoring initiatives.

However, defining ecologically robust and legally compliant compensatory measures for mobile marine mammal species presents significant challenges. Unlike site-based species, mobile species range widely and interact with multiple pressures across vast and remote areas. This complexity underscores the importance of:

- A strategic and evidence-based approach to marine mammal compensation; and
- Sufficient baseline data collection, to ensure measures are targeted, effective and deliver measurable conservation outcomes.

Ultimately, compensation must not only address the specific impacts of a project but must also demonstrably maintain or restore the functional coherence of the wider protected site network.

[39] Noting that at the date of this book, Hornsea 4 is on hold.

CASE STUDY – THE MORAY FIRTH SAC

The Moray Firth SAC illustrates how site protection can extend beyond designated boundaries to safeguard highly mobile marine species such as bottlenose dolphins. Although the SAC was originally designated to protect a geographically localised population, research continues to show that these dolphins' range widely along the east coast of Scotland and England (and in some instances, individuals and small groups have been sighted further afield). Importantly, the SAC's conservation objectives and accompanying guidance explicitly recognise the functional connectivity between the site and wider marine areas, meaning that activities occurring beyond the SAC boundaries must also be assessed for their potential impacts on the protected population. This case study demonstrates that the implementation of the various Habitats Regulations can provide dynamic and population-level protection, where sufficient scientific evidence exists to inform management. It offers a valuable model for the protection of other mobile species – such as harbour porpoise – highlighting the importance of long-term monitoring and a management approach that reflects the ecological realities of a species range.

The conservation objectives for the bottlenose dolphins in the Moray Firth SAC are set out below:[40]

> *"1. To ensure that the qualifying features of the Moray Firth SAC are in favourable condition and make an appropriate contribution to achieving Favourable Conservation Status.*
>
> *2. To ensure that the integrity of the Moray Firth SAC is maintained or restored in the context of environmental changes by meeting objectives 2a, 2b and 2c for each qualifying feature:*

[40] NatureScot, *Conservation and Management Advice, Moray Firth SAC*, June 2025, Annex 1. Available here: https://www.nature.scot/sites/default/files/special-area-conservation/8327/conservation-and-management-advice.pdf.

For bottlenose dolphin

2a. The population of bottlenose dolphin is a viable component of the site.

2b. The distribution of bottlenose dolphin throughout the site is maintained by avoiding significant disturbance.

2c. The supporting habitats and processes relevant to bottlenose dolphin and the availability of prey for bottlenose dolphin are maintained."

The conservation objective that *"the population of bottlenose dolphin is a viable component of the site"* is central to the SAC's importance, and Annex 1 of the NatureScot Conservation and Management Advice for the Moray Firth SAC[41] provides further information.

This population of bottlenose dolphins has been the subject of detailed research since 1989, carried by the University of Aberdeen in collaboration with the Sea Mammal Research Unit at the University of St Andrews. This long-term photo-identification and monitoring work has demonstrated that the bottlenose dolphin population range well beyond the SAC boundary, using a broader area that includes the Coastal East Scotland (CES) Management Unit. Because of this, the SAC population is considered to be equivalent to the CES Management Unit population.

Recent data indicate that the abundance of bottlenose dolphins in the CES Management Unit is 226 individuals (214-239 with a 95% confidence interval). This estimate is derived from a weighted mean of annual population estimates from 2020 – 2022, as reported by *Cheney et al.* (2024).[42] Importantly, despite some year-to-year variation, the

41 NatureScot, *Conservation and Management Advice, Moray Firth SAC*, June 2025, Annex 1.

42 Cheney, B.J., Arso Civil, M., Hammond, P.S. and Thompson, P.M. 2024. *Site Condition Monitoring of bottlenose dolphins within the Moray Firth Special*

number of dolphins using the Moray Firth SAC between 2001 and 2022 appears to be stable. In addition, trends suggest that the overall population along the east coast of Scotland is increasing. Notably, more than 50% of this population use the SAC annually, underscoring the site's continued relevance and conservation value.

Consequently, conservation objective 2a, that the population of bottlenose dolphins is a viable component of the site, seeks to minimise the risk to bottlenose dolphins from injury or killing posed by activities, whether these occur within or outside the SAC. In this context, 'significant' is interpreted to mean "*impacts that affect bottlenose dolphin such that recovery cannot be expected.*"

Given that bottlenose dolphins are highly mobile, their long-term maintenance in the SAC is intrinsically linked to their ability to access and use habitat and prey resources beyond the SAC, in areas that are functionally linked. Therefore: "*When assessing the effects of any plan or project, consideration should therefore be given to whether impacts out with the SAC could affect achievement of this Conservation Objective.*"

The Moray Firth SAC case study offers a compelling example of how the Habitats Regulations can be applied to protect a mobile marine species at the population level. While the SAC was originally established to safeguard a geographically localised group of bottlenose dolphins, decades of dedicated research have demonstrated that these dolphins' range widely across the east coast of Scotland and into northern England. As a result, any proposed development within the wider range of this population that is likely to have a significant effect on the SAC will trigger the need for an Appropriate Assessment.

Crucially, the way in which the National Site Network has been implemented here means that the SAC affords protection to the entire population throughout its functional range – not just within the

---

Area of Conservation: 2017 – 2022. NatureScot Commissioned Report No. 1360.

boundaries of the site. This exemplifies a more ecologically meaningful approach, which is only possible due to the long-term, individual-level monitoring of the population, which has created an exceptional evidence base for management and regulatory decision-making.

This case therefore raises a wider question: can the same approach be applied to other mobile species, such as harbour porpoise, where site-based protection is more challenging still? Achieving comparable protection would require a similarly strategic and science-led approach, underpinned by robust data on distribution, movement and population dynamics. As such, the Moray Firth SAC provides a valuable model – not just for the conservation of bottlenose dolphins – but for advancing the protection of other marine species across the UK's National Site Network.

STRATEGIC COMPENSATION AND THE ENERGY ACT 2023: A NEW FRAMEWORK FOR OFFSHORE WIND DEVELOPMENT

A significant recent development in the UK's legal framework for marine environmental protection – and one with direct implications for HRA – is the introduction of Part 13 of the Energy Act 2023, which establishes a new statutory basis for strategic compensation in relation to offshore wind development. This framework forms part of the Offshore Wind Environmental Improvement Package and introduces new concepts and mechanisms that may transform how compensatory measures for adverse effects on integrity of European marine sites are designed, delivered and assessed.

Application and scope

The framework under Part 13 applies exclusively to "*relevant offshore wind activities*",[43] a defined term encompassing both project-level actions – such as the planning, construction, operation or decommissioning of offshore wind electricity infrastructure – and broader strategic planning activities, including the identification of suitable areas for future development, whether or not any particular offshore wind electricity infrastructure is in contemplation. "*Offshore wind electricity infrastructure*" is defined to include generating stations, in the UK marine area, that generate electricity from wind, or infrastructure, in the UK marine area, used or intended for use in connection with an offshore wind generating station, or the conveyance of electricity generated by an offshore wind generating station.[44]

Accordingly, these new provisions are geographically confined to the UK marine area and do not apply to other types of marine development.

Strategic compensation

At the heart of this new regime is section 291, which enables public authorities to discharge their environmental compensation obligations arising from HRAs through the delivery of "strategic compensation".

Strategic compensation under section 291 may be delivered in anticipation of, or in response to, the cumulative impacts of one or more offshore wind projects. Public authorities are empowered to "bank" compensatory measures – such as habitat creation or restoration – that have already been delivered or are planned and then allocate these measures against their obligations for individual development projects. These measures need not be delivered at the same location as the impact site.

43 Energy Act 2023, section 290(1).

44 Energy Act 2023, section 290(2) and (3).

This mechanism is intended to reduce the need for bespoke, project-by-project compensatory arrangements under the various Habitats Regulations, instead enabling a more strategic, centralised approach.

Marine Recovery Fund

To operationalise the strategic compensation model, section 292 provides for the creation of one or more Marine Recovery Funds. These funds, to be established via Regulations, are intended to finance the delivery of strategic compensation measures across multiple projects and spatial scales.

The Secretary of State is granted broad discretion to determine the structure, governance and operation of these funds. In principle, this creates a pathway for collective investment in ecological recovery.

Future regulations on assessment and compensation

Section 293 confers additional regulatory powers on the Secretary of State to develop a bespoke system for the assessment of environmental effects and compensatory measures in the context of relevant offshore wind activities.

Crucially, the Regulations enabled by section 293 may disapply or modify core provisions of existing environmental law, including those under the various Habitats Regulations in England, Wales, Scotland and Northern Ireland.

This raises the prospect of a parallel, potentially less stringent assessment regime for offshore wind projects, decoupled from the procedural and substantive requirements of the various Habitats Regulations. The precise content of any new Regulations remains to be determined, but the enabling powers under section 293 are expansive and include provisions such as:

- specifying the matters to be dealt with by an assessment;

- the procedure to be followed in carrying out an assessment, including when an assessment must be carried out and matters that must be taken into account;
- when or how compensatory measures must or may be provided; and
- disapplying or otherwise modifying, whether generally or in specified circumstances or subject to specified conditions, any of the provisions listed in the respective HRA sections of the various Habitats Regulations (as set out above).

SUMMARY

In summary, the HRA process remains a cornerstone of legal protection for European marine sites, requiring competent authorities to assess and avoid adverse effects on site integrity before authorising plans or projects. The legal framework sets out a stepwise set of tests: consideration of likely significant effects, appropriate assessment, consideration of alternative solutions, and – where no alternative solutions exists and imperative reasons of overriding public interest apply – the securing of compensatory measures.

However, recent legislative developments under the Energy Act 2023 introduce a new and potentially transformative framework for the delivery of compensatory measures in the context of offshore wind development. These changes reflect a clear policy direction aimed at enabling the expansion of offshore wind while maintaining environmental safeguards. However, they also raise important legal and practical questions: for example, how will coherence and ecological effectiveness of compensation be secured at scale? What does strategic compensation mean for accountability, public participation and legal certainty? And to what extent will the new regime maintain the integrity of the HRA's underlying principles? These are crucial issues that must be addressed as the UK navigates the twin imperatives of accelerating renewable energy deployment and safeguarding its most ecologically valuable marine sites and species.

CHAPTER FOUR

ENVIRONMENTAL IMPACT ASSESSMENT AND MARINE MAMMALS

INTRODUCTION

While the Habitats Regulations Assessment applies specifically to European sites, including Special Areas of Conservation designated for marine mammals, many marine activities fall under a broader environmental assessment framework: the Environmental Impact Assessment (**EIA**) regime. EIA applies to a wide range of projects, regardless of proximity to designated sites, and requires developers to assess the potential effects of their proposals on the environment – including on marine mammals.

Importantly, the EIA regime covers all marine mammal species, not just those associated with SACs, and the legal thresholds, processes and outcomes under EIA differ significantly from those under HRA (covered in Chapters 3 and 5).

EIA is a critical legal process designed to ensure that the environmental implications of development proposals are identified, assessed and taken into account before any development consent is granted.

The EIA regime in the UK is derived from the European Union's EIA Directives, the most recent of which is Directive 2014/52/EU of 16 April 2014 (**EIA Directive**). The EIA Directive requires Member States to ensure that public or private projects that are likely to have significant effects on the environment are subject to an environmental assessment before development consent is given.

As set out in Chapter 3, "Project" is defined in the EIA Directive as:

> *" – The execution of construction works or of other installations or schemes,*
>
> - *Other interventions in the natural surroundings and landscape including those involving the extraction of mineral resources."*

Accordingly, the EIA Directive applies to a wide range of projects, which are specified in its Annexes I and II.

This chapter outlines the legal framework for EIA in the UK, with a focus on marine mammal impacts from marine and coastal developments.

IMPLEMENTATION OF THE EIA DIRECTIVE IN THE UK

The EIA Directive is implemented in the UK through a number of parallel regimes, each applying to different types of development and consenting processes. While the most widely known is the regime for Town and Country Planning, governed by local planning authorities, this is only one of many frameworks established to give effect to the EIA Directive.

Other marine-specific regimes exist and may apply depending on the nature of the project. The below list identifies some of the key EIA regulations currently in force across the UK and which are relevant to the impacts of development on marine mammals.

- Town and Country Planning (Environmental Impact Assessment) Regulations 2017 (SI 2017/571) (**EIA Regulations 2017**)
- Town and Country Planning (Environmental Impact Assessment) (Wales) Regulations 2017 (SO 2017/567)

- The Town and Country Planning (Environmental Impact Assessment) (Scotland) Regulations 2017 (SSI 2017/102)
- The Planning (Environmental Impact Assessment) Regulations (Northern Ireland) 2017 (SI 2017/83)
- Infrastructure Planning (Environmental Impact Assessment) Regulations 2017 (SI 2017/572) (**NSIP EIA Regulations 2017**)
- The Electricity Works (Environmental Impact Assessment) (England and Wales) Regulations 2017 (SI 2017/580), as amended by The Electricity Works (Environmental Impact Assessment) (England and Wales) (Amendment) (Wales) Regulations 2019 (SI 2019/292)
- The Marine Works (Environmental Impact Assessment) (Scotland) Regulations 2017 (SSI 2017/115)
- The Electricity Works (Environmental Impact Assessment) (Scotland) Regulations 2017 (SSI 2017/101)
- The Marine Works (Environmental Impact Assessment) Regulations 2007 (SI 2007/1518), as amended by The Marine Works (Environmental Impact Assessment) (Amendment) Regulations 2017 (SI 2017/588) and by The Marine Works (Environmental Impact Assessment) and Marine Strategy (Amendment) Regulations 2018 (SI 2018/287)
- Offshore Petroleum Production and Pipe-lines (Assessment of Environmental Effects) Regulations 1999 (SI 1999/360), Pipe-line Works (Environmental Impact Assessment) Regulations 2000 (SI 2000/1928, and Public Gas Transporter Pipe-line Works (Environmental Impact Assessment) Regulations 1999 (SI 1999/1672), all of which have been amended by the Offshore Petroleum Production and Pipe-lines (Environmental Impact

Assessment and other Miscellaneous Provisions) (Amendment) Regulations 2017 (SI 2017/582)

- Water Resources (Environmental Impact Assessment) (England and Wales) Regulations 2003 (SI 2003/164) (as amended by the Water Resources (Environmental Impact Assessment) (England and Wales) (Amendment) Regulations 2017 (SI 2017/583)

- Harbour Works (Environmental Impact Assessment) Regulations 1999 (SI 1999/3445) and Harbour Works (EIA) (Amendment) (England and Wales) Regulations 2009 (SI 2009/269)

- Environmental Impact Assessment (Miscellaneous Amendments Relating to Harbours, Highways and Transport) Regulations 2017 (SI 2017/1070)

The remainder of this chapter will focus on the regimes under the EIA Regulations 2017 and the NSIP EIA Regulations 2017 as these provide examples that are very applicable to impacts of development on marine mammals.

WHAT IS AN ENVIRONMENTAL IMPACT ASSESSMENT?

An EIA is the structured process through which information about the potential environmental effects of a proposed development are identified, evaluated and made available to decision-makers, consultees and the public before consent is given. At its core is the preparation of an Environmental Statement, which must be submitted to the relevant authority.

EIAs differ from Strategic Environmental Assessments, which evaluate the environmental impact of plans and programmes at a broader strategic level, whereas EIAs relate to individual projects.

When is an EIA required?

Determining whether the proposed development falls under the scope of an 'EIA development' is a crucial early step in the planning process. This is because the relevant consenting authority cannot grant planning permission or development consent for an EIA development unless an EIA has been conducted.

An EIA is required for developments that fall within the scope of the applicable EIA Regulations. For example, in accordance with the EIA Regulations 2017, an EIA must be done if a development falls within Schedule 1. Schedule 1 developments are usually over a certain size and include a wide range of projects, including:

- Nuclear power stations and other nuclear reactors (except research installations for the production and conversion of fissionable and fertile materials, whose maximum power does not exceed 1 kilowatt continuous thermal load);[1]

- Trading ports, piers for loading and unloading connected to land and outside ports (excluding ferry piers) which can take vessels of over 1,350 tonnes;[2]

- Extraction of petroleum and natural gas for commercial purposes where the amount extracted exceeds 500 tonnes per day for petroleum or 500,000 cubic metres per day for gas;[3] and

---

1 Town and Country Planning (Environmental Impact Assessment) Regulations 2017, Schedule 1, paragraph 2(2).

2 Town and Country Planning (Environmental Impact Assessment) Regulations 2017, Schedule 1, paragraph 8(2).

3 Town and Country Planning (Environmental Impact Assessment) Regulations 2017, Schedule 1, paragraph 14.

- Pipelines with a diameter of more than 800mm and length of more than 40km for the transport of gas, oil or chemicals; or carbon dioxide for the purposes of geological storage, including associated booster stations.[4]

Schedule 3 of the EIA Regulations 2017 sets out the selection criteria for screening Schedule 2 developments and includes factors such as the characteristics and location of the development. In particular, the environmental sensitivity of geographical areas likely to be affected by development must be considered, including coastal zones and the marine environment, European sites (including SACs for marine mammals) and other areas classified or protected under national legislation, for example SSSIs.

Examples of EIA Regulations 2017, Schedule 2 developments which are relevant to marine mammals include:

- Intensive fish farming where the installation resulting from the development is designed to produce more than 10 tonnes of dead weight fish per year;

- Reclamation of land from the sea;

- Extraction of minerals by fluvial or marine dredging;

- Installations for the harnessing of wind power for energy production (wind farms) where the development involves the installation of more than 2 turbines; or the hub height of any turbine or height of any other structure exceeds 15 metres;

[4] Town and Country Planning (Environmental Impact Assessment) Regulations 2017, Schedule 1, paragraph 16.

- Construction of harbours and port installations including fishing harbours (unless included in Schedule 1) where the area of works exceeds 1 hectare;

- Coastal work to combat erosion and maritime works capable of altering the coast through the construction, for example, of dykes, moles, jetties and other sea defence works, excluding the maintenance and reconstruction of such works; and

- Marinas where the area of the enclosed water surface exceeds 1000 square metres.

Whether a Schedule 2 development requires an EIA is determined on a case-by-case basis through a screening process, which considers whether the development is likely to have significant environmental effects. Developers may request a screening opinion from the planning authority, for example, the local planning authority or the Secretary of State, but such a request is not mandatory.

Responsibility for conducting an EIA

The developer wishing to undertake a project is responsible for doing an EIA, but it must be prepared by a competent expert such as an environmental consultant. The developer can ask the relevant planning authority for guidance on what the Environmental Statement should cover. This guidance is known as a scoping opinion if it is given by the local planning authority, or a scoping direction if it is given by the Secretary of State.

KEY STAGES IN THE EIA PROCESS

The EIA process includes several key stages:

1. **Screening** – if a developer is unsure whether their development requires an EIA, they can (but are not obliged to) ask the planning authority for a screening decision.

2. **Scoping** – this determines what issues need to be considered in the Environmental Statement. If a developer is unsure what should be included in an Environmental Statement, they can (but are not obliged to) ask the planning authority for a scoping opinion or a scoping direction.

3. **Preparation and submission of an Environmental Statement** – the developer must put together an Environmental Statement and submit this to the planning authority alongside their application for planning permission.

4. **Consultation with statutory consultees, the public and interested third parties** – the planning authority needs to take account of the Environmental Statement and any representations made about the development by the relevant consultation bodies (for example, the Environment Agency, Natural England or the JNCC), the public and any interested third parties before it can decide whether to grant planning consent. The relevant EIA Regulations contain provisions on how the Environmental Statement, and any further information requested by the planning authority, should be publicised and made available to the relevant consultation bodies, the public and interested third parties. The specific requirements depend on when during the planning process the Environmental Statement is submitted. The aim of these provisions is to ensure that those wishing to comment on the impact of the development on the environment are given a reasonable opportunity to do so.

5. **Decision on whether to grant planning consent** – when the planning authority makes its decision, it must make the following information available to the public:

    a. The reasons for granting or refusing the planning consent and, where consent is granted, any conditions attached to it;

    b. Any mitigation measures that will be required to avoid, reduce or offset the environmental impacts of the development; and

    c. How the decision can be challenged.

The process is not strictly linear. For instance, a developer may omit screening if it is obvious that an EIA is required or combine screening and scoping into a single request. Additionally, if a planning application is submitted without an Environmental Statement and the planning authority determines that an EIA is needed, the developer must provide the Environmental Statement at a later stage.

NATIONALLY SIGNIFICANT INFRASTRUCTURE PROJECTS (NSIPS) IN ENGLAND

The Planning Act 2008 created a system of development consent for major infrastructure projects, referred to as Nationally Significant Infrastructure Projects (**NSIPs**) in England. The types of projects that may qualify as NSIPs are set out in section 14 of the Planning Act 2008 and include the construction or extension of a generating station[5] and the construction or alteration of harbour facilities, which are relevant to marine mammals.[6] Further information about generating stations is provided in section 15 of the Planning Act 2008 and includes offshore

5 Planning Act 2008, section 14(1)(a).

6 Planning Act 2008, section 14(1)(j).

generating stations with capacity of more than 100 megawatts,[7] which will cover most large offshore energy projects, including wind farms.

NSIPs require development consent from the Secretary of State. Applications for development consent are known as development consent order (**DCO**) applications. The NSIP EIA Regulations 2017 set out the requirements for EIAs for DCO applications in England.

Development listed in Schedule 1 to the NSIP EIA Regulations 2017 will always require an EIA. There are no thresholds or criteria set out in Schedule 2 to the NSIP EIA Regulations 2017. Whether an EIA is needed for such Schedule 2 developments will need to be considered on a case-by-case basis using the criteria set out in Schedule 3 to determine if the development will have a significant impact on the environment.

WHAT SHOULD AN ENVIRONMENTAL STATEMENT INCLUDE?

An Environmental Statement must include the information required by the relevant EIA Regulations (for example, the content specified in Schedule 4 of the EIA Regulations 2017). The specific environmental effects that must be addressed will generally be those identified through the most recent scoping process, where the developer has requested a scoping opinion or direction – although this step is not mandatory.

Typically, an Environmental Statement will consist of a series of technical reports prepared by specialist ecological and environmental consultants, assessing the likely significant effects of the proposed development.

The following list, taken from Schedule 4 of the EIA Regulations 2017 provides an example of some of the key information that is required to

---

7 Planning Act 2008, section 15(3).

be included in an Environmental Statement relevant to marine mammals:

- A description of the development including:
  - a description of the location of the development;
  - a description of the physical characteristics of the whole development;
  - a description of the main characteristics of the operational phase of the development (in particular any production process), for instance, energy demand and energy used, nature and quantity of the materials and natural resources (including water, land, soil and biodiversity) used;
  - an estimate, by type and quantity, of expected residues and emissions (such as water, air, soil and subsoil pollution, noise, vibration, light, heat, radiation and quantities and types of waste produced during the construction and operation phases).
- A description of the reasonable alternatives, for example in terms of development design, technology, location, size and scale, and an indication of the main reasons for selecting the chosen option, including a comparison of the environmental effects;
- A description of the relevant aspects of the current environment (baseline scenario) and an outline of the likely evolution thereof without implementation of the development as far as natural changes from the baseline scenario can be assessed with reasonable effort on the basis of the availability of environmental information and scientific knowledge;

- A description of the factors likely to be significantly affected by the development, including fauna and flora;

- A description of the likely significant effects of the development on the environment resulting from, among other things:

  - the construction and existence of the development, including, where relevant, demolition works;

  - emissions of pollutants, noise, vibration;

  - the use of natural resources;

  - risks to the environment, for example due to accidents or disasters;

  - the cumulation of effects with other existing and/or approved projects, taking into account any existing environmental problems relating to areas of particular environmental importance likely to be affected;

  - the impact of the project on the climate and the vulnerability of the project to climate change;

  - the technologies and the substances used.

- The description of the likely significant effects should cover the direct effects and any indirect, secondary, cumulative, transboundary, short-term, medium-term and long-term, permanent, temporary, positive and negative effects of the development.

- A description of the forecasting methods or evidence, used to identify and assess the significant effects on the environment, including details of difficulties (for example, lack of knowledge) encountered compiling the required information and the main uncertainties involved;

- A description of the measures envisaged to avoid, prevent, reduce, or if possible, offset any identified significant adverse effects on the environment; and any proposed monitoring arrangements (for example the preparation of a post-project analysis). That description should explain the extent to which significant adverse effects on the environment are avoided, prevented, reduced or offset and should cover both the construction and operational phases.

- Finally, a non-technical summary of the information above. This is essential for members of the public and other interested parties to be able to access the information.

In relation to marine mammals, Environmental Statements play a critical role in identifying and mitigating potential adverse effects arising from proposed developments. Marine mammals are highly sensitive to environmental changes, particularly underwater noise, which can disrupt communication, navigation, feeding, and breeding behaviours. Common issues that arise during EIA for these species include the assessment of noise impacts from construction activities such as pile driving, vessel traffic, and operational noise. Additionally, risks related to habitat degradation, pollution, and the cumulative effects of multiple projects in the same region must be carefully evaluated. Addressing these factors through thorough baseline data collection, predictive modelling, and the implementation of robust mitigation and monitoring measures helps ensure that the ecological integrity of marine environments is preserved, and the wellbeing of marine mammal populations is safeguarded.

SUMMARY

EIA is a key legal mechanism for identifying and managing the environmental effects of marine and coastal developments in the UK, including those affecting marine mammals. While it operates independently of HRA, EIA plays a complimentary role by requiring developers to consider impacts on all marine mammal species – not just those associated with protected sites. The process is designed to ensure that significant environmental effects are fully understood and transparently considered before development consent is granted. This is important to marine mammals because it ensures that their habitats and populations are protected from potentially harmful developments, promoting the conservation of biodiversity and the health of marine ecosystems.

CHAPTER FIVE

COMPARING HRA AND EIA IN THE CONTEXT OF MARINE MAMMALS

Although both the Habitats Regulations Assessment (**HRA**) and Environmental Impact Assessment (**EIA**) processes regulate the environmental effects of development, they operate under distinct legal regimes with different objectives, thresholds and consequences. Both are key legal mechanisms for assessment in the UK marine environment, and both are relevant when considering impacts and mitigation for marine mammals.

While HRA and EIA serve different legal purposes and apply under distinct statutory regimes, they share common ground. Both require the early identification of environmental risks, collection of robust baseline data and implementation of effective mitigation measures. In practice, they are often triggered simultaneously, especially in the context of marine development, but they assess impacts in different ways.

This comparison focusses specifically on how each regime applies to marine mammals, highlighting similarities – such as the need to assess potential and cumulative impacts – and key differences, particularly around legal thresholds, species coverage and the consequences for project approval. It is important to identify any potential marine mammal issues early when there remain options in terms of project design.

HRA is a site-based assessment, triggered where a plan or project may affect the integrity of a European site such as a Special Area of Conservation (**SAC**) designated for harbour porpoise, bottlenose dolphin, grey or harbour seals. In contrast, EIA takes a broader approach, requiring assessment of impacts on all marine mammals regardless of their conservation status or whether they occur within designated sites.

A fundamental distinction lies in the legal thresholds and consequences for project approval. HRA, which is outcome-based, imposes a strict precautionary standard: consent must be refused if there is a risk of adverse effects on site integrity unless there are no alternative solutions or imperative reasons of overriding public interest which can be demonstrated. EIA, by contrast, is process-based and is more discretionary in nature. It is primarily an information-gathering tool intended to inform decision-making, rather than impose substantive constraints.

The table below summarises the main areas of overlap and divergence between the two regimes.

Topic	**HRA**	**EIA**
Species scope	Limited to Annex II marine mammals (bottlenose dolphin, harbour porpoise, grey seal and harbour seal) for which SACs have been designated.	Applies to all marine mammals.
Legal test	Must demonstrate no adverse effect on the integrity of the site in light of the site's conservation objectives.	Must identify, describe and assess significant effects on identified receptors, including marine mammals.
Outcome constraint	Cannot proceed if adverse effects cannot be ruled out beyond all reasonable scientific doubt unless derogations met	Can proceed with impacts if deemed acceptable

Basis of assessment	Conservation objectives of protected sites	Broad environmental receptors, including marine mammals.
Legal framework	Conservation led (Habitats Directive)	Planning and development led (EIA Directive)

In summary, while both HRA and EIA play crucial roles in evaluating the environmental implications of marine developments, they offer differing degrees and scopes of protection for marine mammals. The HRA provides a more stringent, precautionary framework, offering robust legal safeguards but limited to only four Annex II marine mammal species, for which SACs have been designated. Conversely, the EIA, although less demanding in its legal tests, encompasses a broader spectrum of marine mammals, ensuring that potential impacts on all species in the vicinity are considered. Together, these frameworks complement each other, with the HRA ensuring strict conservation measures for particular species within designated sites and functionally linked areas, and the EIA providing a comprehensive overview of environmental effects across the wider marine ecosystem.

CHAPTER SIX

THE LEGAL LANDSCAPE OF MARINE MAMMAL DISTURBANCE: CHALLENGES AND INTERPRETATIONS

INTRODUCTION

Disturbance represents one of the most intricate and challenging concepts within the legal framework for marine mammals in the UK. Unlike more tangible offences such as killing or capture, disturbance encompasses a range of behaviours and impacts that are often indirect, subtle and highly context dependent. It requires an integration of science with legal interpretation to assess whether human activities affect marine mammals in ways that compromise their survival, reproduction or natural behaviours.

Under the Habitats Directive, disturbance is a key offence triggering protections for cetaceans, which are classified as European protected species (see Chapter 1). Article 12 prohibits the deliberate disturbance of these species, but the Habitats Directive itself does not provide a definition of what constitutes 'disturbance'. This absence leaves Member States to interpret the concept through a patchwork of guidance documents, case law and national legislation and ensuring that scientific judgment is applied. The European Commission's 2021 guidance offers important clarifications, emphasising that disturbance includes any deliberate actions that may affect survival chances, breeding success or cause displacement of animals, particularly when such impacts extend beyond individuals to population and species levels.

In addition, Article 6 of the Habitats Directive requires Member States to prevent 'significant disturbance' of species in Special Areas of Conservation (**SACs**), focussing on conservation objectives at the site level. The application of this requirement to highly mobile and acoustically sensitive marine mammals presents distinct challenges, especially in relation to underwater noise impacts from human activities.

The various Habitats Regulations reflect these EU principles, but also introduce variations, including the criminalisation of 'reckless' disturbance in Scotland, and detailed guidance on assessing the significance of noise disturbance against conservation objectives of harbour porpoise SACs.

Despite these legal frameworks and scientific advances, uncertainty persists over how to define and regulate disturbance in practice. The thresholds for legal offences remain contested, especially for temporary or non-lethal impacts. Licensing regimes provide some defences but are often encumbered by grey areas.

This chapter delves into the legal framework addressing disturbance in the context of marine mammals. It discusses specific legal provisions, case studies, and regulatory mechanisms in place within the UK.

DISTURBANCE AND THE PROTECTION OF MARINE MAMMALS UNDER THE HABITATS DIRECTIVE

Article 12: Deliberate disturbance of Annex IV(a) species

As discussed in Chapter 1, Article 12 of the Habitats Directive establishes a 'system of strict protection' for species listed in Annex IV(a), which includes all cetaceans. Member States are required to take requisite measures to prohibit "deliberate disturbance", particularly during sensitive periods such as breeding and migration.[1]

The various Habitats Regulations all provide a 'definition' of 'disturbance'.[2]

Under The Conservation of Habitats and Species Regulations 2017, as amended and the Conservation of Offshore Marine Habitats and Species Regulations 2017, as amended:

> *"... disturbance of animals includes in particular any disturbance which is likely –*
>
> *(a) to impair their ability –*
>
> > *(i) to survive, to breed or reproduce, or to rear or nurture their young; or*
> >
> > *(ii) in the case of animals of a hibernating or migratory species, to hibernate or migrate; or*
>
> *(b) to affect significantly the local distribution or abundance of the species to which they belong."*

In Scotland, under The Conservation (Natural Habitats, &c.) Regulations 1994, as amended:

> *"It is an offence –...*

---

1 Habitats Directive, Article 12(1)(b).

2 The Conservation of Habitats and Species Regulations 2017, regulation 43(2); The Conservation of Offshore Marine Habitats and Species Regulations 2017, regulation 45(2); The Conservation (Natural Habitats, etc.) Regulations (Northern Ireland) 1995, regulation 34(1)(c); The Conservation (Natural Habitats, &c.) Regulations 1994, regulation 39(b)(v) and (vi).

(b) deliberately or recklessly – …

(v) to disturb such an animal in a manner that is, or in circumstances which are, likely to significantly affect the local distribution or abundance of the species to which it belongs;

(vi) to disturb such an animal in a manner that is, or in circumstances which are, likely to impair its ability to survive, breed or reproduce, or rear or otherwise care for its young;"

In Northern Ireland, under The Conservation (Natural Habitats, etc.) Regulations (Northern Ireland) 1995, as amended:

"It is an offence –

(c) deliberately to disturb such an animal in such a way as to be likely to –

(i) affect the local distribution or abundance of the species to which it belongs;

(ii) to impair its ability to survive, breed or reproduce, or rear or care for its young; or

(iii) impair its ability to hibernate or migrate;"

In October 2021, the European Commission adopted a guidance document[3] (**2021 Guidance**) providing interpretation and clarifications on Article 12 of the Habitats Directive. The 2021 Guidance plays an important role in shaping Member States' understanding of the concept

---

3 Commission Notice C(2021) 7301, *Guidance document on the strict protection of animal species of Community interest under the Habitats Directive*, C(2021) 7301. Available here: https://op.europa.eu/en/publication-detail/-/publication/a17dbc76-2b51-11ec-bd8e-01aa75ed71a1/language-en

of 'disturbance' and its implications for European protected species, including cetaceans.

The 2021 Guidance explains that disturbance should be understood broadly, encompassing any activity that deliberately disturbs a species to the extent that it may affect its chances of survival, breeding success or reproductive ability, or leads to a reduction in the occupied area or the relocation or displacement of the species.[4]

The 2021 Guidance goes further, stating:

> "*(2-38) Considering their specific life histories (in particular their reproductive strategy or mobility) and the often complex social interactions of some animals, disturbance of individuals can often have impacts on population levels, for example, this would be the case if disturbing a pregnant female or separating a mother from calf of large, long-living and highly mobile marine animals with low fecundity, such as marine mammals.*
>
> *(2-39) Generally, the intensity, duration and frequency of repetition of disturbances are important parameters when assessing their impact on a species. Different species will have different sensitivities or responses to the same type of disturbance, which has to be taken into account. Factors causing disturbance for one species might not create disturbance for another. Also, the sensitivity of a single individual of a certain species might be different depending on the season or on certain periods in its life cycle (e.g. breeding period).*
>
> *(2-40) A case-by-case approach is therefore required. The competent authorities will have to reflect carefully on the level of disturbance that is to be considered harmful, taking into account the specific characteristics of the species concerned and the situation, as explained*

[4] Commission Notice C(2021) 7301, *Guidance document on the strict protection of animal species of Community interest under the Habitats Directive*, C(2021) 7301, paragraph 2.3.2.a (2-37).

above. For instance, repeated disturbance of cetaceans by whale-watching boats could lead to significant impacts on individual specimens, with negative consequences for the local population. On the other hand, sporadic disturbances without any likely negative impact on the individual animal or local population, such as for example scaring away a wolf from entering a sheep enclosure in order to prevent damage, should not be considered as disturbance under Article 12."

The 2021 Guidance also draws attention to the growing concern over anthropogenic underwater noise and its potential to disturb cetaceans, stating as follows:[5]

"14 – Further guidance: Addressing the impacts of underwater anthropogenic noise on cetaceans

Activities that can cause disturbance of strictly protected marine species, such as cetaceans, include shipping or offshore windfarms through continuous noise and construction, oil and gas exploration, or military activities through impulsive noise. The consequences for cetaceans range from disturbance and masking of the sound used in communication, to short and long-term hearing impairment, physical injuries and even death. Combined with the additional effects of stress, confusion and panic, this can be devastating for individual animals and for whole populations.

As regards shipping, Member States can consider a wide range of preventative measures, including reducing the speed of vessels or rerouting the traffic. Concerning seismic surveys using airguns or offshore construction using pile driving, these activities usually require permits. Therefore, for such plans and projects, the necessary preventative measures can be proposed in the context of environmental

---

5 Commission Notice C(2021) 7301, *Guidance document on the strict protection of animal species of Community interest under the Habitats Directive*, C(2021) 7301, paragraph 2.3.2.a.

impact assessments under the Strategic Environmental Assessment and Environmental Impact Assessment directives.

The challenges in defining appropriate mitigation measures have been recognised on the international level and relevant methodological guidelines have been adopted, for example by ACCOBAMS and ASCOBANS focusing on cetaceans, while the Convention on Migratory Species produced guidelines on environmental impact assessments for marine noise-generating activities. These guidance documents provide a very useful framework for ensuring compliance with the rules under the Habitats Directive. However, their application should always take into account the latest scientific and expert knowledge in the field and should be based on detailed considerations of each particular activity and its effects on particular species."

Finally, the 2021 Guidance reiterates that for a disturbance to fall within the scope of Article 12(1)(b), it must be deliberate. According to the interpretation provided in relation to Article 12(1)(a), an action is considered deliberate if the person carrying it out either intended the prohibited consequence (such as the killing or capturing of a specimen) or at least accepted the possibility that it might occur.[6] This sets a relatively high threshold under Article 12. However, some national regimes take a stricter approach. In Scotland, for example, "reckless" disturbance is also an offence, allowing for enforcement even where intent or acceptance cannot be established.

[6] Commission Notice C(2021) 7301, *Guidance document on the strict protection of animal species of Community interest under the Habitats Directive*, C(2021) 7301, paragraph 2.3.1.

The interpretation of 'Disturbance' under Article 12(1)(b) – Lessons from *Morge v Hampshire County Council*

A key authority on the interpretation of Article 12(1)(b) of the Habitats Directive is the UK Supreme Court's judgment in *Morge v Hampshire County Council.*[7] While the case related to the potential disturbance of bats, the Supreme Court's analysis of the Habitats Directives provisions remains directly relevant to the protection of other European protected species, including cetaceans.

Lord Brown, delivering the leading judgment, articulated several core principles that guide how 'disturbance' should be understood under Article 12(1)(b). Importantly, the Court emphasised that this provision provides specific protection to species, not merely to their habitats. As Lord Brown put it at paragraph 19 of the judgment:

> *"First, that it is an article affording protection specifically to species and not to habitats, although obviously, as here, disturbance of habitats can also indirectly impact on species."*

This distinction is vital in the context of marine mammals, where many threats, such as underwater noise, are not physically destructive to habitats but can nonetheless cause profound disturbance at the species level.

Lord Brown also stressed that Article 12(1)(b) protects the species as a whole, not merely individual specimens:

> *"Secondly, and perhaps more importantly, the prohibition encompassed in article 12(1)(b), in contrast to that in 12(1)(a), relates to the protection of 'species', not the protection of 'specimens of these species'."*

[7] *Morge v Hampshire County Council* [2011] UKSC 2.

This wider focus aligns with ecological thinking about population-level impacts and reinforces that disturbance must be assessed in terms of its consequences for the viability and conservation status of the species in a given area, not just on individuals.

One of the most important parts of the judgment concerns how significance is treated. Although Article 12(1)(b) does not explicitly require that disturbance be 'significant', Lord Brown clarified that a qualitative assessment of impact is still necessary:

> *"Thirdly, whilst it is true that the word 'significant' is omitted from article 12(1)(b) – in contrast to article 6(2) and, indeed, article 12(4) which envisages accidental capture and killing having a "significant negative impact on the protected species" – that cannot preclude an assessment of the nature and extent of the negative impact of the activity in question upon the species and, ultimately, a judgment as to whether that is sufficient to constitute a 'disturbance' of the species."*

In other words, the legal threshold for disturbance is not met by any minor or transient disruption. There must be a sufficient negative impact, particularly one that interferes with the species' ability to breed, rear young, hibernate or migrate. This is especially pertinent for marine mammals, whose seasonal behaviours and reliance on acoustic cues make them particularly vulnerable to certain types of anthropogenic disturbance.

Further, the timing and biological sensitivity of the species must be considered:

> *"Fourthly, it is implicit in Article 12(1)(b) that activity during the period of breeding, rearing, hibernation and migration is more likely to have a sufficient negative impact on the species to constitute prohibited 'disturbance' than activity at other times."*

For migratory species, like many cetaceans, this aspect underscores the need to understand and mitigate activities during key life-cycle phases, reinforcing the importance of seasonality in licensing and enforcement decisions.

In paragraph 22 of the judgment, Lord Brown also drew attention to conservation-related factors that competent authorities should consider when assessing whether disturbance is prohibited:

> *"Two further considerations can, I think, usefully be identified to be borne in mind by the competent authorities deciding these cases (considerations which seem to me in any event implicit in the Commission's Guidance). First (and this I take from a letter recently written to the respondent by Mr Huw Thomas, Head of the Protected and Non-Native Species Policy at DEFRA, the Department responsible for policy with regard to the Directive): "Consideration should . . . be given to the rarity and conservation status of the species in question and the impact of the disturbance on the local population of a particular protected species. Individuals of a rare species are more important to a local population than individuals of more abundant species. Similarly, disturbance to species that are declining in numbers is likely to be more harmful than disturbance to species that are increasing in numbers."*

This passage provides clear support for a context-sensitive approach, where the same activity may constitute unlawful disturbance for one species (e.g., an endangered population) but not for another, more resilient population with more stable numbers. It reflects a precautionary ethos consistent with the purpose of the Habitats Directive.

In summary, *Morge* illustrates that disturbance under Article 12(1)(b) involves more than mere interference: it must be understood in terms of population-level effects, conservation status, ecological sensitivity and timing. For marine mammals, the judgment reinforces the need the robust scientific assessment and a nuanced, species-specific analysis when evaluating potential impacts from development or other activities.

Article 6: Disturbance in Special Areas of Conservation (SACs)

Whereas Article 12 protects European protected species wherever they occur in their natural range, Article 6 applies only to Annex II species, for which SACs are designated. Among marine mammals, only the harbour porpoise, bottlenose dolphin, grey and harbour seals are listed in Annex II.

Article 6(2) of the Habitats Directive requires that:

> *"Member States shall take appropriate steps to avoid, in the special areas of conservation, the deterioration of natural habitats and the habitats of species as well as disturbance of the species for which the areas have been designated, in so far as such disturbance could be significant in relation to the objectives of this Directive."*

The European Commission's 2018 Natura 2000 guidance, as discussed in Chapter 3[8] (**Natura 2000 Guidance**) discusses what could constitute *significant* disturbance of a species in a European site. Significant disturbance, as clarified in the Natura 2000 Guidance, does not directly affect the physical conditions of a site; instead, it concerns the species themselves. Disturbances can be limited in time, such as noise or light pollution, but their significance depends on several key factors, including intensity, duration and frequency of occurrence. These parameters are critical in evaluating whether an activity or event crosses the threshold into significant disturbance.

The Natura 2000 Guidance goes on to advise that in order to evaluate whether disturbance is significant in relation to the objectives of the Habitats Directive, reference can be made to Article 1(i) of the definition

8 Commission Notice C(2018) 7621 final, Brussels, 21.11.2018, *Managing Natura 2000 sites. The provisions of Article 6 of the 'Habitats' Directive 92/43/EEC.* Paragraph 3.5.2. Available here: https://op.europa.eu/en/publication-detail/-/publication/11e4ee91-2a8a-11e9-8d04-01aa75ed71a1

of the favourable conservation status of a species. This evaluation considers three primary factors:

1. Firstly, population dynamics data on the species concerned – if an event, activity or process contributes to the long-term decline of a population of the species within a site, it may be deemed a significant disturbance. This includes any impact that undermines the species' ability to maintain itself on a long-term basis as a viable element of its natural habitat.

2. Secondly, natural range – a disturbance is considered significant if it contributes to a reduction, or risk of reduction, in the natural range of the species within the site.

3. Thirdly, habitat availability – any event, activity or process that contributes to the reduction of the size of the available habitat of the species can be considered significant disturbance.

The Natura 2000 Guidance highlights specific effects such as noise, vibrations and the isolation of sub-populations of a species as being capable of causing significant disturbances for that species. Therefore, the failure of a Member State to implement appropriate measures to prevent such disturbances constitutes a failure to fulfil its obligations under Article 6(2) of the Habitats Directive.

Importantly, the assessment of disturbance significance is nuanced. Factors such as the intensity, frequency and duration of the disturbance must be considered, as their impacts can vary between species and under different environmental conditions. For instance, the presence of adequate undisturbed areas nearby, or fluctuations in food resources can influence the severity of the disturbance's impact.

In summary, disturbances that contribute to the long-term decline of a species' population, reduce its range or diminish its habitat within a European site must be carefully assessed within the framework of the site's conservation objectives. This approach ensures that the integrity of the Natura 2000 network (National Site Network) is maintained.

Case study: Harbour porpoise SACs

In 2020, the JNCC, Natural England and the Department of Agriculture, Environment and Rural Affairs (**DAERA**) in Northern Ireland issued guidance (**JNCC Guidance**) on significant disturbance thresholds within harbour porpoise SACs in England, Wales and Northern Ireland.[9]

The JNCC Guidance recognises that a number of noise generating activities can potentially result in disturbance and injury to harbour porpoise, and gives examples, including geophysical surveys for oil and gas exploration, the detonation of unexploded ordnance, Acoustic Deterrent Devices, pile driving undertaken for the installation of offshore wind turbines and the construction of marine facilities such as harbours.

The JNCC Guidance defines noise disturbance within a harbour porpoise SAC from a plan / project, individually or in combination, as significant if it excludes harbour porpoises from more than:

- 20% of the relevant area[10] of the site in any given day;[11] or

9 JNCC (2020). Guidance for assessing the significance of noise disturbance against Conservation Objectives of harbour porpoise SACs (England, Wales & Northern Ireland). JNCC Report No. 654, JNCC, Peterborough, ISSN 0963-8091. https://data.jncc.gov.uk/data/2e60a9a0-4366-4971-9327-2bc409e09784/JNCC-Report-654-FINAL-WEB.pdf

10 The JNCC 2020 guidance defines the 'relevant area' as '*that part of the SAC that was designated on the basis of the highest persistent densities for that season (summer defined as April to September inclusive, winter as October to March inclusive).*'

11 The JNCC 2020 guidance states that '*To be considered within the Habitats Regulation Assessment and, if needed, licence conditions should ensure that daily thresholds are not exceeded. Day to day monitoring of compliance is not*

- an average of 10% of the relevant area of the site over a season.[12]

The JNCC Guidance goes on to reiterate that any plan or project which, individually or in combination, could breach these area / time thresholds could be deemed to have an adverse effect on site integrity necessitating noise management measures such as adjustment of activity schedules, the use of alternative technologies and noise abatement, and that the aim of noise management should be to keep below the thresholds as much as possible.

These thresholds are designed to ensure that porpoises retain sufficient access to habitat and are not displaced from key foraging or resting areas. Recognising the high variability in porpoise distribution, the JNCC Guidance emphasises the need for site-level assessment, using Effective Deterrence Ranges[13] to quantify temporary habitat loss based on empirical data.

The JNCC Guidance also underlines the complexity of regulating marine activities, the adaptive nature of the approach, and the importance of incorporating new scientific evidence to refine thresholds and mitigation.

In September 2024, NatureScot published its Conservation and Management Advice for the Inner Hebrides and the Minches SAC. This includes the Conservation Objective that '*The distribution of harbour porpoise throughout the site is maintained by avoiding significant*

---

practicable and therefore retrospective compliance monitoring is required to test whether the licence conditions are being adhered to.'

12 The JNCC 2020 guidance defines summer as April to September inclusive, and winter as October to March inclusive. The guidance gives an example: '*a daily footprint of 19% for 95 days would result in an average of 19x95 / 183 days (summer) = 9.86%.*'

13 Effective Deterrence Range refers to the spatial extent, typically a radius around a noise source, within which marine animals such as harbour porpoise are likely to be disturbed or deterred by underwater noise.

disturbance', however, it does not provide significant disturbance thresholds similar to that in the JNCC Guidance.

Case study: Bottlenose dolphins in the Moray Firth SAC

As discussed in Chapter 3, one of the Conservation Objectives for the bottlenose dolphin designated feature of the Moray Firth SAC is that:

> *"2b. The distribution of bottlenose dolphin throughout the site is maintained by avoiding significant disturbance."*[14]

Annex 1 of NatureScot's Conservation and Management Advice for the Moray Firth SAC provides further detail on the interpretation of 'significant disturbance' in the context of these bottlenose dolphins, stating:

> *"Interpretation of 'significant disturbance' will depend on the context, including the information that is provided through the plan or project, and is then subject to the appraisal to assess risk. It should be interpreted to mean disturbance that affects the integrity of the site through alteration of the distribution of bottlenose dolphin within the SAC such that recovery cannot be expected or effects can be considered long term. Bottlenose dolphin calves are highly dependent on their mothers for up to 2 years therefore prolonged disturbance is more likely to constitute significant disturbance and to have an impact on site integrity. It is expected that significant disturbance will lead to more than a transient effect on the distribution of bottlenose dolphin. It may result in the following effects:*

[14] NatureScot, *Conservation and Management Advice, Moray Firth SAC*, June 2025, Annex 1. Available here: https://www.nature.scot/sites/default/files/special-area-conservation/8327/conservation-and-management-advice.pdf.

- *Contributes to the long-term decline in the use of the site by bottlenose dolphin.*

- *Changes to the distribution of bottlenose dolphin on a continuing or sustained basis.*

- *Changes to bottlenose dolphin behaviour such that it reduces the ability of the species to survive, breed or rear their young.*

For example, a localised, short term disturbance away from the coast may not be considered to cause levels of disturbance that would raise concern, whereas continual disturbance close to shore or in a key foraging area.

The factors limiting recovery in terms of the distribution of bottlenose dolphin within the site include, the timing and duration of the activity (e.g. summer months when calving is thought to occur); the overlap of the activity with areas used by dependent mothers and calves; and the ability of bottlenose dolphin to still access sufficient food whilst they are subject to disturbance."

LICENCES FOR DISTURBANCE

Both the assimilated EU law (the various Habitats Regulations) and primary national legislation (the Wildlife and Countryside Act 1981 and the Wildlife (Northern Ireland) Order 1985) provide licencing regimes under which activities that would otherwise constitute offences – including disturbance of protected marine mammals – may be lawfully carried out.

These licensing regimes allow for the lawful disturbance of marine protected species in specific, controlled circumstances. For instance, species licences may be granted to permit close approaches to cetaceans in the course of scientific research, such as when conducting photo-identification studies of animals. They may also be required for survey work involving protected species, or for development activities that will affect such species. The nature of the proposed activity, and whether the species is protected under European or national legislation, determines which licensing regime applies and the level of scrutiny that follows.

Licensing regime – European Protected Species

The following regulations under the various Habitats Regulations provide a defence to the offences discussed in Chapter 1, if the act is carried out in accordance with the terms of a licence granted for a number of specific purposes:

- Regulation 55 of the Conservation of Habitats and Species Regulations 2017;
- Regulation 55 of the Conservation of Offshore Marine Habitats and Species Regulations 2017;
- Regulation 44 of the Conservation (Natural Habitats, &c.) Regulations 1994; and
- Regulation 39 of the Conservation (Natural Habitats, etc.) Regulations (Northern Ireland) 1995.

These purposes, as relevant to marine mammals, include:

- Scientific or educational purposes;[15]

---

[15] Conservation of Habitats and Species Regulations 2017, regulation 55(2)(a); The Conservation of Offshore Marine Habitats and Species Regulations 2017, regulation 55(1)(d); The Conservation (Natural Habitats, &c.) Regulations 1994, regulation 44(2)(a) (which also includes 'research'); The Conservation (Natural Habitats, etc.) Regulations (Northern Ireland) 1995, regulation 39(2)(a).

- Preventing serious damage to fisheries;[16]

- In the interests of public health or public safety[17] or for other imperative reasons of overriding public interest, including those of a social or economic nature and beneficial consequences of primary importance for the environment.[18]

Such a licence must only be granted if the relevant licensing body is satisfied that:

(a) There is no satisfactory alternative;[19] and

(b) The action authorised will not be detrimental to the maintenance of the population of the species concerned at a favourable conservation status in their natural range.[20]

---

[16] Conservation of Habitats and Species Regulations 2017, regulation 55(2)(g); The Conservation of Offshore Marine Habitats and Species Regulations 2017, regulation 55(1)(b); The Conservation (Natural Habitats, &c.) Regulations 1994, regulation 44(2)(g); The Conservation (Natural Habitats, etc.) Regulations (Northern Ireland) 1995, regulation 39(2)(g).

[17] The Conservation of Offshore Marine Habitats and Species Regulations 2017, regulation 55(1)(a).

[18] Conservation of Habitats and Species Regulations 2017, regulation 55(2)(e); The Conservation (Natural Habitats, &c.) Regulations 1994, regulation 44(2)(e); The Conservation (Natural Habitats, etc.) Regulations (Northern Ireland) 1995, regulation 39(2)(e).

[19] The Conservation of Offshore Marine Habitats and Species Regulations 2017, regulation 55(2).

[20] Conservation of Habitats and Species Regulations 2017, regulation 55(9); The Conservation (Natural Habitats, &c.) Regulations 1994, regulation 44(3); The Conservation (Natural Habitats, etc.) Regulations (Northern Ireland) 1995, regulation 39(3).

Notably *"satisfactory alternative"* is not defined in any of the Regulations, nor clarified in statutory guidance, leaving scope for interpretation and case-by-case decision-making.

The relevant licensing body varies by jurisdiction:

- In England, for activities of scientific or educational purposes, within the English inshore region (seaward of mean low water mark), the Marine Management Organisation is the competent authority;[21] elsewhere, the authority is Natural England.[22]

- In England, where the purpose is for preserving public health or safety, or other imperative reasons of overriding public interest, or where the purpose is to prevent serious damage to fisheries, the relevant licensing body is the Secretary of State.[23]

- In Wales, the relevant licensing body is Natural Resources Wales.[24]

- In Scotland, for licences for scientific or conservation purposes, it is the appropriate nature conservation body;[25] for licences for preventing damage to fisheries or for preserving public health or

[21] Note that they will rely on Natural England for assistance with licensing decisions.

[22] The Conservation of Habitats and Species Regulations 2017, regulation 58(2).

[23] The Conservation of Habitats and Species Regulations 2017, regulation 58(3) and (4), and regulation 3(1).

[24] The Conservation of Habitats and Species Regulations 2017, regulation 58(5).

[25] The Conservation (Natural Habitats, &c.) Regulations 1994, regulation 44(4)(a).

safety or other imperative reasons of overriding public interest, the authority is the agriculture Minister.[26]

- In Northern Ireland, the 'Department' (being DAERA), is responsible for granting licences.[27]

- Offshore, the 'relevant administration' responsible for granting licences are the Secretary of State, the Scottish Ministers and the Welsh Ministers.[28]

In practice, species licences for disturbance are typically required for scientific research that involves approaching animals at close range. For example, researchers conducting photo-identification studies of cetaceans may need to manoeuvre a vessel in close proximity to the animals, which could constitute a disturbance offence if carried out without a licence. Similarly, tagging studies or biopsy sampling will very likely be considered disturbance and would need to be licenced under the scientific purposes listed above.

By contrast, activities such as marine ecotourism, recreational wildlife watching from boats or paddleboarding and jet-skiing in known marine mammal habitats – while potentially disturbing – may not fall within one of the listed licensing purposes. This would need to be considered carefully by parties participating in these activities.

[26] The Conservation (Natural Habitats, &c.) Regulations 1994, regulation 44(4)(b).

[27] The Conservation (Natural Habitats, etc.) Regulations 1995, regulation 39(1).

[28] The Conservation of Offshore Marine Habitats and Species Regulations 2017, regulation 55(15).

Licensing regime – Nationally Protected Species

The following sections under the WCA 1981 and the Wildlife (Northern Ireland) Order 1995 provide a defence to the offences discussed in Chapter 1, if the act is carried out in accordance with the terms of a licence granted for a number of specific purposes:

- Section 16(3) WCA 1981; and
- Article 18(1) Wildlife (Northern Ireland) Order 1995.

These purposes include:

- For scientific or educational purposes;[29]
- For scientific, research or educational purposes;[30]
- For the purpose of photography;[31]
- For the purpose of preserving public health or public safety;[32]
- For the purpose of preventing serious damage to fisheries;[33]
- In England, for reasons of overriding public interest.[34]

---

29 Wildlife and Countryside Act 1981, section 16(3)(a).

30 The Wildlife (Northern Ireland) Order 1985, Article 18(1)(a).

31 Wildlife and Countryside Act 1981, section 16(3)(e); The Wildlife (Northern Ireland) Order 1995, Article 18(1)(b).

32 Wildlife and Countryside Act 1981, section 16(3)(f); The Wildlife (Northern Ireland) Order 1995, Article 18(1)(d).

33 Wildlife and Countryside Act 1981, section 16(3)(h).

34 Wildlife and Countryside Act 1981, section 16(3)(j).

The addition of section 16(3)(j) by the Environment Act 2021 introduces a new licensing purpose for "*reasons of overriding public interest*" in England only. While this provision is widely regarded as primarily aimed at enabling development, the term is not defined in statute. It could possibly be interpreted to include commercial activities such as ecotourism, for example, where such an activity would generate income in a small community. Importantly, this provision has not been extended to Wales or Scotland and thus does not provide a ground for licensing in those jurisdictions.

Further, the Environment Act 2021 introduced additional licencing tests for England only through section 16(3B). This section states that:

> *"In England, the appropriate authority shall not grant a licence under subsection (3) unless it is satisfied – (d) that there is no other satisfactory solution; and (e) that the grant of the licence is not detrimental to the survival of any population of the species of animal or plant to which the licence relates."*

These additional tests are aimed at aligning the WCA 1981 licensing regime with that under the various Habitats Regulations, providing a more coherent approach in England.

In Northern Ireland, a licence may not be granted that permits the killing, injuring or taking of seals for the purpose of preventing damage to fisheries (see Chapter 7).[35]

SUMMARY

The concept of 'disturbance' under the Habitats Directive is central to the legal protection of marine mammals in UK waters, but its definition is context-dependent and remains open to interpretation. Article 12 prohibits deliberate disturbance of species, focusing on impacts to

[35] The Wildlife (Northern Ireland) Order 1995, Article 18(3ZA).

survival and reproduction, whereas Article 6 addresses significant disturbance within SACs where it may affect site integrity or conservation objectives. In practice, disturbance of marine mammals poses significant challenges in legal interpretation, given the scientific uncertainties, species-specific responses and variable spatial and temporal patterns of exposure.

Licensing regimes exist to authorise certain activities that would otherwise be unlawful. However, these regimes apply only in narrow circumstances and do not readily accommodate many activities that may be considered to cause disturbance to marine mammals.

CHAPTER SEVEN

LEGAL FRAMEWORKS FOR MARINE MAMMAL BYCATCH AND ENTANGLEMENT

INTRODUCTION

Bycatch – the unintentional capture of non-target species during fishing operations – poses a significant and direct threat to marine mammals globally and in the UK. It can affect all populations and species of marine mammal, with small cetaceans such as harbour porpoise and common dolphins, and pinnipeds being particularly susceptible. In addition, entanglement – often associated with static nets and abandoned fishing gear, is a significant risk to all marine mammal species.

The UK is required to monitor, report, and mitigate incidental capture of marine mammals through domestic and EU-derived fisheries and conservation legal instruments. However, as highlighted in the EFRA Committee Report, despite these obligations, the scale, frequency, and long-term impacts of bycatch and entanglement in UK waters remain inadequately documented and understood, and subsequently, poorly managed (discussed in Chapter 9). Evidence presented during the EFRA Committee inquiry suggests that current bycatch levels may be unsustainable for certain populations, raising serious conservation and welfare concerns. The EFRA Committee's findings reflect a growing recognition that the UK's regulatory framework, while comprehensive on paper, as discussed in this chapter, has struggled to deliver meaningful outcomes in practice.

This chapter examines the current legal and regulatory mechanisms governing marine mammal bycatch in the UK. It begins with an analysis of the Fisheries Act 2020, the UK's principal post-Brexit fisheries legislation, which establishes the statutory frameworks for sustainable fishing and the conservation of marine ecosystems. The chapter then considers the continued relevance of assimilated EU law, as well as the role of fishing vessel licence conditions, bycatch monitoring schemes, and the potential applicability of nature conservation law, particularly the various Habitats Regulations, in relation to bycatch incidents.

THE LEGAL FRAMEWORK FOR BYCATCH IN UK FISHERIES LAW

The Fisheries Act 2020

The Fisheries Act 2020 provides the foundation of UK domestic fisheries law following Brexit. It sets out a series of high-level objectives which guide fisheries policy, including several provisions relevant to the issue of marine mammal bycatch.

Among the eight overarching objectives in the Fisheries Act 2020, the ecosystem objective is of primary relevance. Section 1(4) of the Fisheries Act 2020 provides that:

> *"(a) fish and aquaculture activities are managed using an ecosystem-based approach so as to ensure that their negative impacts on marine ecosystems are minimised and, where possible, reversed; and (b) incidental catches of sensitive species are minimised and, where possible, eliminated."*

The term "ecosystem-based approach" is defined in section 1(10) as:

> *"an approach which –*
>
> *(a) ensures that the collective pressure of human activities is kept within levels compatible with the achievement of good environmental status (within the meaning of the Marine Strategy Regulations 2010 (S.I. 2010/1627)), and*

> *(b) does not compromise the ability of marine ecosystems to respond to human-induced changes;"*

The concept of 'sensitive species', crucial to bycatch considerations, is defined in section 52 and includes, in the context of marine mammals:

> *"(a) any species of animal or plant listed in Annex II or IV of the Habitats Directive"*

This encompasses all cetaceans (which are listed in Annex IV(a)), as well as the grey and common seals (which are listed in Annex II). The definition also extends to:

> *"any other species of animal or plant, other than a species of fish, whose habitat, distribution, population size or population condition is adversely affected by pressures arising from fishing or other human activities."*

Additional fisheries objectives reinforce the need to address bycatch. The "bycatch objective", in section 1(6), provides that:

> *"(a) the catching of fish that are below minimum conservation reference size, and other bycatch, is avoided or reduced;*
>
> *(b) catches are recorded and accounted for; and*
>
> *(c) bycatch that is fish is landed, but only where this is appropriate and (in particular) does not create an incentive to catch fish that are below minimum conservation reference size."*

Further relevant objectives include the "sustainability objective", which includes in section 1(2) that:

> *"(a) fish and aquaculture activities are –*
>
> > *(i) environmentally sustainable in the long term,"*

And the "scientific evidence objective", at section 1(5), which provides that:

> *"(a) scientific data relevant to the management of fish and aquaculture activities is collected;*
>
> *(b) where appropriate, the fisheries policy authorities work together on the collection of, and share, such scientific data; and*
>
> *(c) the management of fish and aquaculture activities is based on the best available scientific advice."*

In addition, the "precautionary objective" is found in section 1(3) and includes that:

> *"(a) the precautionary approach to fisheries management is applied,"*

The "precautionary approach to fisheries management" is defined in section 1(10) as:

> *"an approach in which the absence of sufficient scientific information is not used to justify postponing or failing to take management measures to conserve target species, associated or dependent species, non-target species or their environment."*

While these objectives set a strong legal and policy framework, the Fisheries Act 2020 itself does not create directly enforceable duties in relation to bycatch of marine mammals. Rather, it relies on policy instruments – most notably the Joint Fisheries Statement[1] – to give practical effect to these objectives.

Published in November 2022 in compliance with section 2 of the Fisheries Act 2020, the Joint Fisheries Statement sets out how the

1 https://www.gov.uk/government/publications/joint-fisheries-statement-jfs

fisheries policy authorities[2] intend to meet the fisheries objectives. In particular, it provides important clarification on how the ecosystem-based approach is to be implemented.

In relation to the "ecosystem objective", the Joint Fisheries Statement confirms that:

> *"The fisheries policy authorities will achieve, or contribute to the achievement of, the ecosystem objective and GES [good environmental status] through management regimes which maintain or, where required, recover, protect and improve the health of marine ecosystems. Such management approaches will be designed to minimise the impacts of fishing on the environment beyond individual stocks, such as damage to seabed habitats and bycatch of sensitive species and non-target species, while allowing appropriate human uses of our seas for the benefit of current and future generations."*[3]

Of particular relevance to reducing bycatch of marine mammals, the Joint Fisheries Statement confirms that:

> *"The national fisheries authorities are committed to working with the fishing industry to meet the ecosystem objective to minimise and, where possible, eliminate the unwanted bycatch and entanglement of sensitive species including cetaceans… and seals…. The fisheries policy authorities recognise that bycatch is one of the most significant threats to these species, and an important part of meeting the sustainability objective is that fisheries activities are environmentally sustainable in the long term."*[4]

---

2 Defined in section 52 of the Fisheries Act 2020 as the Secretary of State, the Scottish Ministers, the Welsh Ministers and the Northern Ireland department.

3 Joint Fisheries Statement, paragraph 2.1.13.

4 Joint Fisheries Statement, paragraph 4.2.8.4.

It also refers to the UK Bycatch Mitigation Initiative,[5] which outlines how the UK will seek to meet the ambitions of the ecosystem objective:

> *"The UK Bycatch Mitigation Initiative (BMI) published in August 2022 outlines how the fisheries policy authorities will achieve the ambitions of the ecosystem objective by improving our understanding through scientific monitoring and research, identifying bycatch "hotspots' of high risk, developing and adopting effective mitigation measures, supporting fishers to implement mitigation measures, and working with international partners to reduce bycatch of sensitive species globally. Actions in the BMI include investing in bycatch monitoring programmes to fill knowledge gaps and diversify monitoring techniques, targeting monitoring and mitigation towards bycatch "hotspots", scaling up use of effective mitigation measures, and supporting the development of new technologies and approaches where appropriate such as deterrents, technical modification to gears and alternative gears. These policies and actions will also help achieve the scientific evidence objective through the collection and sharing of data relevant to the management of fisheries and basing management decisions on the best available scientific advice. Fisheries policy authorities will set out the next steps towards implementation of the BMI."*[6]

Finally, the Bycatch Mitigation Initiative itself clarifies the responsibilities of each fisheries policy authority, stating:

> *"Each fisheries policy authority (as defined in s52 of the Fisheries Act) is responsible for setting out how they will take action on bycatch, for example through implementation plans. In future, where fisheries*

---

[5] https://www.gov.uk/government/publications/marine-wildlife-bycatch-mitigation-initiative/marine-wildlife-bycatch-mitigation-initiative

[6] Joint Fisheries Statement, paragraph 4.2.8.5.

policy authorities decide to implement new measures to reduce bycatch in fisheries, this will follow consultation processes as appropriate."[7]

In summary, the Fisheries Act 2020 and its associated policy instruments contain multiple references to the need to minimise and, where possible, eliminate bycatch of marine mammals. However, the absence of legally binding targets or enforceable measures means that the effectiveness of these provisions depends on the political will and administrative follow-through of the relevant authorities.

Assimilated EU Law: Regulation 2019/1241 on the Conservation of Fisheries Resources and the Protection of Marine Ecosystems through Technical Measures[8] (Technical Measures Regulation)

The Technical Measures Regulation remains an important component of UK law as assimilated EU legislation. It was retained and amended post-Brexit by the Common Fisheries Policy and Animals (Amendment etc.) (EU Exit) Regulations 2019/1312 (**CFP Regulations**). The Technical Measures Regulation lays down technical measures relating to the taking and landing of marine biological resources, the operation of fishing gear, and the interaction of fishing activities with marine ecosystems. It applies to activities undertaken by UK fishing vessels within the fishing zones defined in Article 5 of the Technical Measures Regulation, as well as by fishing vessels flying the flag of, and registered in, third countries when fishing in UK waters. Some of the Articles of the

---

7 Bycatch Mitigation Initiative, Executive Summary.

8 Regulation (EU) 2019/1241 of the European Parliament and of the Council of 20 June 2019 on the conservation of fisheries resources and the protection of marine ecosystems through technical measures, amending Council Regulations (EC) No 1967/2006, (EC) No 1224/2009 and Regulations (EU) No 1380/2013, (EU) 2016/1139, (EU) 2018/973, (EU) 2019/472 and (EU) 2019/1022 of the European Parliament and of the Council, and repealing Council Regulations (EC) No 894/97, (EC) No 850/98, (EC) No 2549/2000, (EC) No 254/2002, (EC) No 812/2004 and (EC) No 2187/2005

Technical Measures Regulation, including Article 11 (see below) also apply to recreational fishing.

The objectives of the Technical Measures Regulation, insofar as they are relevant to marine mammals, are set out in Article 3 and include:

> *"1. Technical measures shall contribute to the achievement of the fisheries objectives.*
>
> *2. Technical measures shall in particular contribute to the following objectives:*
>
>> *… (b) ensure that incidental catches of sensitive marine species, including those listed under Directives 92/43/EEC [the Habitats Directive] and 2009/147/EC, that are a result of fishing, are minimised and where possible eliminated so that they do not represent a threat to the conservation status of these species;*
>>
>> *(c) ensure, including by using appropriate incentives, that the negative environmental impacts of fishing on marine habitats are minimised;*
>>
>> *(d) have in place fisheries management measures for the purpose of complying with the Marine Strategy Regulations 2010 and any enactment giving effect to Directives 92/43/EEC or 2000/60/EC, in particular with a view to achieving good environmental status"*

While this reflects the ambition set out in the "ecosystem objective" of the Fisheries Act 2020 – that incidental catches of sensitive species are *"minimised and, where possible, eliminated"* – it is qualified in the Technical Measures Regulation by the requirement that such catches must not *"represent a threat to the conservation status"* of the species concerned.

Article 4 of the Technical Measures Regulation sets a 'target', stating that:

> *"1. Technical measures shall aim to ensure that…*

> *(b) incidental catches of marine mammals… do not exceed levels provided for in legislation applicable in any part of the United Kingdom and international agreements that are binding on the United Kingdom."*

However, the CFP Regulations have removed the original obligation from the Technical Measures Regulation to review and report on progress made towards achieving this target, thereby potentially weakening the regulatory feedback loop.

Article 11 of the Technical Measures Regulation deals explicitly with the incidental catch of marine mammals and contains several key provisions. First, it prohibits *"the catching, retention on board, transhipment or landing"* of all cetaceans and the grey and common seals.[9] Where such species are caught, it is mandated that such species *"shall not be harmed and specimens shall be promptly released."*[10] An exception is made which allows for the retention on board, transhipment, or landing of *accidentally* caught cetaceans and seals *"as far as this activity is necessary to secure assistance for the recovery of the individual animals and to allow for scientific research on incidentally killed specimens, provided that the competent authorities of the fisheries administration concerned have been fully informed in advance as soon as possible after the catch and in accordance with the relevant assimilated direct legislation."*[11]

Furthermore, Article 11(4) provides that *"On the basis of the best available scientific advice a fisheries administration may, by regulations, put in place mitigation measures or restrictions on the use of certain gear. Such measures shall minimise, and where possible eliminate, the catches of [all cetaceans and grey and harbour seals] and must be at least as stringent as technical measures applicable under relevant assimilated direct legislation."*[12] These measures

9 Regulation 2019/1241, Article 11(1).

10 Regulation 2019/1241, Article 11(2).

11 Regulation 2019/1241, Article 11(3).

12 Regulation 2019/1241, Article 11(4).

must also aim to achieve the targets set out in Article 4(1)(b) of the Technical Measures Regulation.[13]

It is important to note that the CFP Regulations removed provisions from the Technical Measures Regulation requiring fisheries administrations to inform other EU Member States of the measures adopted, and to make appropriate information publicly available.[14] This change may affect transparency and the sharing of best practices across jurisdictions, which had previously been a feature of EU cooperation on marine mammal bycatch mitigation.

While the Technical Measures Regulation sets out high-level objectives to minimise and, where possible, eliminate incidental catches of marine mammals, its practical effectiveness is undermined by a lack of enforceable targets and accountability mechanisms. The requirement that bycatch must not threaten the conservation status of protected species introduces a vague and reactive threshold, rather than a clear, precautionary standard. Although Article 4 references compliance with levels provided for in applicable UK legislation and binding international agreements,[15] the removal of the obligation to review and report on progress towards bycatch targets has weakened transparency and hindered regulatory oversight. Similarly, the discretionary nature of mitigation measures under Article 11 – reliant on action by individual fisheries administrations – and the absence of legal consequences for failing to adopt or implement such measures, limits enforceability. The removal of obligations to share information with other states further reduces opportunities for cooperative monitoring and best practice sharing. Overall, while the Technical Measures Regulation retains strong rhetoric on bycatch reduction, its implementation framework lacks the

---

[13] Regulation 2019/1241, Article 11(5).

[14] CFP Regulations, regulation 5(4)(b).

[15] There are currently no specific numerical bycatch limits for marine mammals in the UK.

legal precision, enforceability and oversight necessary to drive meaningful change in practice.

MONITORING AND REPORTING OBLIGATIONS

Fisheries Licences and the requirement to report bycatch

In 2021, the MMO placed a condition into all fishing vessel licences requiring vessels to report incidents where a vessel's fishing activities have caused or contributed to marine mammal injury or death, or where marine mammals have been caught as bycatch, within 48 hours of the end of a fishing trip. As well as bycatch, this includes any interactions with marine mammals resulting in injury or death whilst searching for fish, shooting or setting gear, towing or hauling gear, taking catch on board, or from entanglement in ropes or lines. The MMO guidance on *Marine Mammal Reporting Requirements*[16] (**MMO Guidance**) states that the reason for the collection of this information is:

> *"To continue to export fisheries products to the United States (US), and to assist conservation efforts in mitigating marine mammal bycatch, the UK needs to comply with international standards for the conservation of marine mammals. This licence condition was introduced to help gather the relevant information to help the UK demonstrate compliance with these standards."*

The MMO Guidance includes a template for reporting, which provides that:

> *"In accordance with fishing vessel licences, any incidents of incidental mortality, injury or bycatch of marine mammals including seals,*

[16] Marine Management Organisation guidance on *Marine Mammal Reporting Requirements*. Available at: https://www.gov.uk/guidance/marine-mammal-reporting-requirements#:~:text=In%202021%2C%20the%20MMO%20placed,end%20of%20a%20fishing%20trip.

dolphins, porpoises and whales caused by or contributed to by commercial fishing operations in the UK EEZ, and for UK vessels operating in international waters, must be reported to the MMO."

This requirement applies to all commercial fishing operations in the UK EEZ, regardless of whether the bycatch occurs in coastal areas or in more remote offshore locations. The duty to report extends not only to direct bycatch, but also where such harm is *contributed to* by fishing operations.

While this mandatory reporting represents a step forward in aligning with international standards and contributing to broader conservation efforts, its practical effectiveness remains uncertain. There are inherent challenges in enforcing compliance, particularly in more remote areas of the EEZ where vessels may not return to UK ports and are less likely to be subject to inspection or oversight. Moreover, awareness of the requirement may be limited among fishers, as the obligation is embedded within lengthy and complex licence documentation that may not be readily accessible or well-understood. Crucially, the condition imposes only a duty to *report* bycatch; there is no corresponding obligation to reduce, mitigate or prevent such bycatch, nor is there any specified consequence for repeated reporting of incidents without follow-up measures.

It is also worth noting that requests for information may be submitted under the Environmental Information Regulations 2004 to the MMO to obtain data on the frequency and nature of such bycatch reports, providing a limited avenue for transparency and scrutiny by civil society, NGOs and other stakeholders.

Monitoring and mitigation under the Habitats Directive

Article 12(4) of the Habitats Directive imposes a specific obligation on Member States to establish a system to monitor the incidental capture and killing of animal species listed in Annex IV(a), which includes all cetacean species. Article 12(4) further requires that, in light of the information gathered, Member States shall take further research or conservation measures as required to ensure that incidental capture and killing does not have a *significant negative impact* on the species concerned.

In the UK, following Brexit, the Habitats Directive continues to apply through the various Habitats Regulations as assimilated EU law. Regulations 52 and 53 of both the Conservation of Habitats and Species Regulations 2017 and the Conservation of Offshore Marine Habitats and Species Regulations 2017 implement the monitoring provisions of Article 12(4) in England and Wales, with parallel provisions in Northern Ireland[17] and in Scotland (in relation to monitoring only).[18]

Despite the clear obligations of Article 12(4), the UK's implementation falls short of what the Habitats Directive requires. Although some monitoring occurs through specific projects (e.g., strandings programmes and limited observer schemes), there is no comprehensive, systematic monitoring scheme in place to assess bycatch levels across all UK fisheries. The current system relies heavily on voluntary or opportunistic data, particularly from strandings networks and limited bycatch observer projects. As such, there is likely insufficient data on the scale of marine mammal bycatch. This was reiterated by the EFRA Committee Report which identified that current levels of bycatch monitoring are insufficient to gain an accurate picture of the numbers of marine mammals killed or injured as a result of bycatch (see Chapter 9).

Furthermore, the reactive element of Article 12(4) – that further measures should be taken to ensure that there is no significant negative impact on the species concerned – has not been effectively triggered in practice. Without robust monitoring data, there is limited scientific basis upon which to determine the need for further conservation or mitigation

[17] The Conservation (Natural Habitats, etc.) Regulations (Northern Ireland) 1995, regulation 36A.

[18] The Conservation (Natural Habitats, &c.) Regulations 1994, regulation 41A.

measures. The lack of precautionary action or adaptive management in the face of uncertainty further undermines the protective intent of the Habitats Directive. In essence, the legal obligation exists on paper, but its implementation in the UK appears fragmented, under-resourced and inadequate to ensure compliance with the underlying objective.

Summary of reporting requirements

The UK's current framework includes reporting obligations under both fisheries licence conditions and the various Habitats Regulations (implementing Article 12(4) of the Habitats Directive), but these mechanisms differ significantly in scope and legal effect.

Under fisheries licences, fishers must report any bycatch of marine mammals within 48 hours of returning from a trip, using a standard MMO reporting template. This requirement applies to all commercial fishing operations within the UK EEZ and by UK vessels operating in international waters. However, the obligation is limited to *reporting only*, without an accompanying legal duty to reduce of prevent bycatch.

Article 12(4) of the Habitats Directive requires that the UK establish a *system of monitoring* and – critically – take *further measures* if the incidental capture and killing of protected species is having a significant negative impact. However, implementation is currently patchy and lacks systematic coverage, meaning that the threshold for triggering conservation measures is rarely, if ever, meaningfully assessed or met. Together, these regimes create a fragmented system of reporting and response, with significant gaps in data, enforcement and action. While they provide a framework for monitoring bycatch, neither currently delivers the proactive, science-based conservation outcomes that the legal frameworks were intended to secure.

POTENTIAL OFFENCES RELATING TO BYCATCH

As discussed in detail in Chapter 1, the UK legal framework establishes multiple regimes under which the capturing, injuring or killing of marine mammals (outcomes which may arise as a result of bycatch) may be considered an offence. However, in some instances, statutory defences are available that can prevent criminal liability. This section examines these offences in the context of bycatch and considers the availability and scope of defences under the primary legal regimes applicable to offences against marine mammals:

1. The Conservation of Offshore Marine Habitats and Species Regulations 2017;
2. The Wildlife and Countryside Act 1981;
3. The Conservation of Habitats and Species Regulations 2017;
4. The Conservation (Natural Habitats &c.) Regulations 1994;
5. The Wildlife (Northern Ireland) Order 1985; and
6. The Conservation (Natural Habitats, etc.) Regulations (Northern Ireland) 1995.

The Conservation of Habitats and Species Regulations 2017 are the principal means through which the Habitats Directive is transposed in England and Wales, including the English inshore region and the Welsh inshore region[19] (broadly, the coastal baseline to 12nm), with The Conservation (Natural Habitats &c.) Regulations 1994 applying in Scotland and The Conservation (Natural Habitats, etc.) Regulations (Northern Ireland) 1995 applying in Northern Ireland inshore regions.

[19] The Conservation of Habitats and Species Regulations 2017, regulations 2(1) and 3(8).

The Conservation of Offshore Marine Habitats and Species Regulations 2017 are the principal means by which the Habitats Directive is transposed in the UK 'offshore marine area',[20] broadly beyond 12nm from the coastal baseline and out to 200nm.

The Conservation of Offshore Marine Habitats and Species Regulations 2017

As discussed in Chapter 1, regulation 45(1) of The Conservation of Offshore Marine Habitats and Species Regulations 2017 prohibits the deliberate capture, injury, killing or disturbing of European protected species, which includes all cetaceans.

Regulation 39 specifies that regulation 45 applies to any person in any part of the waters comprised in the offshore marine area, or on a ship in any part of the waters comprised in the offshore marine area.

However, a statutory defence is available under regulations 45(10) – (12), which provides a legal safeguard for fishers where such outcomes occur, provided specific criteria are met. The wording of these regulations is as follows:

> *"(10) In any proceedings for an offence under paragraph (1), where this paragraph applies the defendant ("D") is not to be taken deliberately to have done anything mentioned in subparagraph (a) [capture, injure, kill], (b) [disturb] or (c) of that paragraph merely because –*
>
> > *(a) D's actions had the result that D did the thing in question; and*

[20] Defined in regulation 2(1) of The Conservation of Offshore Marine Habitats and Species Regulations 2017 as *"(a) any part of the seabed and subsoil situated in any area designated under section 1(7) of the Continental Shelf Act 1964; and (b) any part of the waters within British fishery limits (except the internal waters of, and the territorial sea adjacent to, the United Kingdom, the Channel Islands and the Isle of Man)"*

(b) D intended those actions and knew that they might have that result.

(11) Paragraph (10) applies where the defendant ("D") shows that –

(a) the actions in question were for the purpose, and in the course, of sea fishing;

(b) D did not intend those actions to have the result in question; and

(c) D had taken any steps that could reasonably be taken to ensure compliance with the requirements or conditions of any relevant assimilated law.

(12) In paragraph (11), "any relevant assimilated law" means any instrument relating to sea fishing which –

(a) regulates such fishing for the purpose (whether or not the sole purpose) of minimising the extent to which it has a result of the kind referred to in paragraph (10) or the risk that it may have a result of that kind; and

(b) [transposes an instrument] is adopted by any EU instrument under –

(i) Article 43 of the Treaty on the Functioning of the European Union; or

(ii) Council Regulation (EU) No. 1380/2013 on the Common Fisheries Policy, as amended from time to time or any instrument adopted thereunder."

Key elements of the defence

In order to rely on this defence, a defendant must show that:

1. Fishing was the purpose of their actions (reg 45(11)(a)). The act that resulted in bycatch must have been undertaken for the primary purpose of sea fishing, not for harming marine mammals.

2. There was no intent to cause the result (reg 45(11)(b)). The fisher did not intend to capture, injure, kill or disturb a marine mammal.

3. Reasonable compliance steps were taken (reg 45(11)(c). The fisher had taken all reasonable steps to comply with relevant assimilated law aimed at reducing bycatch, such as gear restrictions, technical measures and mitigation obligations.

Interpretation of "Deliberate" (Reg 45(10))

Subsection 10 clarifies that a person is not to be taken to have acted deliberately (as per the offence under reg 45(1)(a), (b) or (c)), simply because: the defendant's actions (ie sea fishing) had the result that the defendant captured, injured, killed or disturbed a cetacean; and that the defendant intended to engage in the fishing activity and knew that this action might have that result.

This avoids criminalising fishers who take all reasonable precautions but still accidentally catch protected species. It is a recognition of the real-world complexity of sea fishing, where some degree of bycatch risk may be unavoidable even with mitigation in place.

Definition of "Relevant Assimilated Law" (Reg 45(12))

This refers to assimilated EU law from the Common Fisheries Policy (**CFP**), which continues to form part of UK law post-Brexit and includes:

- Technical regulations like gear specifications designed to reduce bycatch (e.g., the Technical Measures Regulation); and

- Measures under CFP Regulation (EU) 1380/2013 aimed at minimising the impact of fishing on non-target species, including protected species.

To benefit from the defence, the fisher must have followed these relevant legal instruments (as assimilated in UK law) to the extent that compliance would reasonably be expected.

Practical implications for marine mammal bycatch

In practice, this means that fishers are not automatically liable for the incidental bycatch of marine mammals in the offshore marine area of the UK (i.e. 12 to 200nm) if they can make out the elements in regulations 45(10) – (12) and demonstrate that:

- their primary purpose was lawful fishing;

- they didn't intend the bycatch; and

- they complied with mitigation requirements under relevant assimilated EU rules, such as using particular technical measures, avoiding certain areas, or following bycatch reduction plans.

However, if a fisher fails to implement available mitigation measures, or continues to fish in a high-risk area despite evidence of repeated bycatch, the defence may not be available. This has particular relevance as more UK-specific bycatch mitigation strategies are developed and incorporated into licence conditions or UK fisheries policy post-Brexit.

Statutory defences under regulation 46

In addition, the following defences set out in regulation 46 are available to the offences in regulation 45:

"46.

(1) A person ("P") is not guilty of the offence under regulation 45(1)(a) of deliberately capturing a wild animal of a European protected species, or an offence under regulation 45(3)(a), if P shows that the act in question –

(a) was in relation to an animal that had been disabled otherwise than by P's unlawful act; and

(b) was done solely for one or both of the purposes of –

(i) tending and releasing it when no longer disabled; or

(ii) releasing it after it had been tended.

(2) A person ("P") is not guilty on an offence under regulation 45(1)(a) or (3)(a) if P shows that the act in question –

(a) was in relation to an animal that had been seriously disabled otherwise than by P's unlawful act and that there was no reasonable chance of its recovering; and

(b) was done solely for one or both of the purposes of

(i) ending the animal's life; or

(ii) disposing of it (otherwise than by sale or exchange) as soon as practicable after it was dead.

…

(7) The defences in paragraphs (1)…. do not apply where it is shown by the prosecution that the defendant's action did not satisfy the conditions in paragraph (8).

(8) Those conditions are that –

> *(a) there was no satisfactory alternative; and*
>
> *(b) the action was not detrimental to the maintenance of the population of the species concerned at a favourable conservation status in their natural range."*

Wildlife and Countryside Act 1981

Under the WCA 1981, an "incidental result" defence is also available in certain circumstances in respect of the offences in section 9 (as discussed in Chapter 1, the offences in section 9(1) of intentionally killing, injuring or taking, and section 9(2) of being in possession or control of any live or dead animal, or anything derived from them, do not apply to cetaceans or to resident pinniped species – they only apply to the walrus).

England and Wales

In England and Wales, section 10(3)(c) WCA 1981 may be applicable in the context of a disturbance offence in respect of whales and dolphins under section 9(4A) WCA 1981. Section 10(3)(c) WCA 1981 provides that:

> *"(3) Notwithstanding anything in section 9, a person shall not be guilty of an offence by reason of...*
>
> *(c) any act made lawful by that section if he shows that the act was the incidental result of a lawful operation and could not reasonably have been avoided."*

This three-limb test requires that: firstly, the act must have been an incidental result; secondly, it must have been to a lawful activity; and thirdly, the result could not have reasonably been avoided.

For the sake of completeness, the following defences set out in section 10(3)(a) and (b) would also apply where a potential offence had taken place in respect of a walrus:

> *"(a) the taking of any such animal if he shows that the animal had been disabled otherwise than by his unlawful act and was taken solely for the purpose of tending it and releasing it when no longer disabled;*
>
> *(b) the killing of any such animal if he shows that the animal had been so seriously disabled otherwise than by his unlawful act that there was no reasonable chance of its recovering."*

Scotland

In Scotland, similar but more detailed defences apply under sections 10(3) and (3A) WCA 1981. Although no cetaceans or resident pinnipeds are offered protection from the offences under section 9, for the sake of completeness, the following defences would apply where a potential offence had taken place in respect of a walrus:

> *"(3) Notwithstanding anything in section 9, a person shall not be guilty of an offence by reason of –*
>
> *(a) The taking of any such animal if he shows that the animal had been disabled otherwise than by his unlawful act and was taken solely for the purpose of tending it and releasing it when no longer disabled;*
>
> *(b) The killing of any such animal if he shows that the animal had been so seriously disabled otherwise than by his unlawful act that there was no reasonable chance of its recovering; or*
>
> *(c) Any act made unlawful by that section ("an unlawful act") if he shows –*
>
> *(i) That each of the conditions specified in subsection (3A) was satisfied in relation to the carrying out of the unlawful act, or*

(ii) That the unlawful act was carried out in relation to an animal bred and, at the time the act was carried out, lawfully held in captivity.

(3A) Those conditions are –

(a) That the unlawful act was the incidental result of a lawful operation or other activity;

(b) That the person who carried out the lawful operation or other activity –

(i) Took reasonable precautions for the purpose of avoiding carrying out the unlawful act; or

(ii) Did not foresee, and could not reasonably have foreseen, that the unlawful act would be an incidental result of the carrying out of the lawful operation or other activity; and

(c) That the person who carried out the unlawful act took, immediately upon the consequence of that act becoming apparent to the person, such steps as were reasonably practicable in the circumstances to minimise the damage or disturbance to the wild animal, or the damage or obstruction to the structure or place, in relation to which the unlawful act was carried out."

The Conservation of Habitats and Species Regulations 2017; The Conservation (Natural Habitats, &c.) Regulations 1994; and The Conservation (Natural Habitats, etc) Regulations (Northern Ireland) 1995 (all as amended)

No equivalent incidental result defences are available under these regimes.

England and Wales

The Conservation (Natural Habitats, &c.) (Amendment) Regulations 2007 (SI 2007/1843) (the '**Amendment Regulations**') amended the Conservation (Natural Habitats, &c.) Regulations 1994 (a previous version of the Conservation of Habitats and Species Regulations 2017) (in England and Wales), as well as making amends to the WCA 1981.

Regulation 7 of the Amendment Regulations amended the WCA 1981 so that European protected species (including all cetaceans) are removed from the scope of certain WCA 1981 offences under section 9. The explanatory notes for the Amendment Regulations state that: "*the Amendment Regulations will... amend the WCA 1981 so that EPS (European protected species) are removed from the scope of certain WCA offences. This ensures that there is no conflict between the two pieces of legislation*"[21] (being the now 2017 Habitats Regulations and the WCA 1981).[22]

The Explanatory Memorandum of the Amendment Regulations elaborates on this, making specific reference to the lack of an incidental result defence in the Habitats Regulations and states that:

> *"With regard to the Amendment Regulations and the changes introduced to the species protection provisions in the Habitats Regulations, the objective is to improve species protection by toughening up and extending the trade rules and creating stronger laws for the protection of such species (animals and plants). The latter objective will be achieved by removing many of the defences available in respect of the offences against EPS. For example, it will no longer be a defence to show that the capturing, killing, destruction or disturbance of wild EPS animals was an incidental and unavoidable result of an otherwise*

[21] Paragraph 4.6 of the Explanatory Memorandum to SI 2007/1843.

[22] It is because of the Amendment Regulations that cetacean species currently do not get the benefit of the offences in section 9(1) WCA 1981.

> *lawful activity... If an activity is likely to result in an offence being committed, those involved will have to consider alternative options or look to avoid impacts. If this is not possible a licence may be required before the activity can be lawfully undertaken..."*[23]

The Explanatory Memorandum does make reference to cetacean bycatch, stating that *"Incidental capture and killing of cetaceans is already widely monitored in UK waters... "*, referring to Statutory Instrument No 17, 2005, The Incidental Catches of Cetaceans in Fisheries (England) Order 2005 (which is now revoked) and The Prevention and Monitoring of Cetacean Bycatch (Scotland) Order 2005 (also now revoked).

The following defences set out in regulation 44 are however available to the relevant offences in regulation 43:

> *"44.—(1) A person ("P") is not guilty of the offence under regulation 43(1)(a) of deliberately capturing a wild animal of a European protected species, or an offence under regulation 43(3)(a) or (b), if P shows that the act in question—*
>
> *(a) was in relation to an animal that had been disabled otherwise than by P's unlawful act; and*
>
> *(b) was done solely for one or both of the purposes of—*
>
> *(i) tending it and releasing it when no longer disabled; or*
>
> *(ii) releasing it after it had been tended.*
>
> *(2) A person ("P") is not guilty of an offence under regulation 43(1)(a) or 43(3)(a) or (b) if P shows that the act in question—*

[23] Paragraph 7.4 of the Explanatory Memorandum to SI 2007/1843.

> *(a) was in relation to an animal that had been seriously disabled otherwise than by P's unlawful act and that there was no reasonable chance of its recovering; and*
>
> *(b) was done solely for one or both of the purposes of—*
>
> > *(i) ending the animal's life; or*
> >
> > *(ii) disposing of it (otherwise than by sale or exchange) as soon as practicable after it was dead."*

Scotland

A similar position was adopted in Scotland as a result of the Conservation (Natural Habitats, &c.) Amendment (Scotland) Regulations 2007 (SSI 2007/80) (the **Scottish Amendment Regulations**).[24]

The Executive Note of the Scottish Amendment Regulations state that the instrument will have the effect of removing the *"existing "incidental result" defence for offences against animals which are EPS ..."*

The following defences set out in regulation 40 are however available to the relevant offences in regulation 39:

> *"40.—(1) A person shall not be guilty of an offence under regulation 39(1)(a) or (b), (2), or (3)(a) or (b), if that person shows that what was done—*
>
> > *(a) was in relation to an animal that had been seriously disabled otherwise than by that person's unlawful act and there was no reasonable chance of its recovering; and*
> >
> > *(b) was done solely for one or more of the purposes of—*

[24] Regulation 28 of SSI 2007/80.

(i) ending the animal's life in a humane manner; or

(ii) where the animal's life had been so ended, disposing of it (otherwise than by sale or exchange) as soon as practicable after it was dead.

(2) A person shall not be guilty of the offence under regulation 39(1)(a) of deliberately or recklessly capturing a wild animal of a European protected species, or an offence under regulation 39(3)(a) or (b), if that person shows that what was done–

(a) was in relation to an animal that had been disabled otherwise than by that person's unlawful act; and

(b) was done solely for one or more of the purposes of—

(i) tending it and releasing it when no longer disabled; or

(ii) releasing it after it had been tended,

and was done in a manner or in circumstances unlikely to cause the animal unnecessary suffering.

(3) A person shall not be guilty of an offence by reason of any act made unlawful by regulation 39 if that person shows that the act was carried out in relation to an animal bred and, at the time the act was carried out, lawfully held in captivity.

(4) The exceptions to regulation 39 in paragraphs (1) and (2) shall not apply where it is shown that–

(a) there was a satisfactory alternative to what was done; or

(b) what was done was detrimental to the maintenance of the populations of the species concerned at a favourable conservation status in their natural range."

Northern Ireland

The following defences set out in regulation 35 are available to the relevant offences in regulation 34 of the Conservation (Natural Habitats, etc.) Regulations (Northern Ireland):

"35.— Exceptions from regulation 34

(1) A person shall not be guilty of an offence under regulation 34(1)(a), (b) or (c) 2 or under regulation 34(2)(a) or (b) if he shows that the contravention in question—

(a) was in relation to an animal that had been seriously disabled otherwise than by his unlawful act and there was no reasonable chance of its recovering, and

(b) was done solely for one or more of the purposes of—

(i) ending the animal's life, or

(ii) disposing if it (otherwise than by sale or exchange) as soon as practicable after it was dead.

(2) A person shall not be guilty of an offence under regulation 34(1) of deliberately capturing a wild animal of a European protected species, or an offence under regulation 34(2)(a) or (b), if he shows that the contravention in question—

(a) was in relation to an animal that had been disabled otherwise than by his unlawful act, and

(b) was done solely for one or more of the purposes of—

(i) tending it and releasing it when no longer disabled, or

(ii) releasing it after it had been tended.

> *(3) The exceptions in paragraphs (1) and (2) shall not apply where it is shown that—*
>
> > *(a) there was a satisfactory alternative to what was done; or*
> >
> > *(b) what was done was detrimental to the maintenance of the population of the species concerned at a favourable conservation status in their natural range."*

As a result, cetacean bycatch within 12 nautical miles of the UK coast, where these respective Regulations apply, may amount to an offence if the constituent elements of the offence are satisfied, no European protected species licence is obtained (and its conditions complied with), and no statutory defence is available.

Pinniped bycatch under the Wildlife (Northern Ireland) Order 1985

Under Article 10(1) of the Wildlife (Northern Ireland) Order 1985, it is an offence to intentionally or recklessly kill, injure or take any wild animal listed in Schedule 5, which includes all pinnipeds (seals), though not cetaceans. Further, under Article 10(4B), it is also an offence to knowingly cause or permit such an act to be carried out by another person.

However, Article 11(3) provides a potential defence to this offence for an *authorised person* (such as a person acting with appropriate authority). This defence applies where:

- The act of killing or injuring the Schedule 5 animal was necessary to prevent serious damage to fisheries, and

- The person notified the Department immediately after taking such action.

Importantly however, this exception is modified in relation to seals by Article 11(3A), as inserted by the Fisheries Act 2020. For seals, the reference to "fisheries" in the list of protected interests is excluded. This means that killing or injuring a seal to protect fisheries (for example, fish stocks or aquaculture operations) is not a valid defence under this provision.

In effect, this amendment narrows the circumstances in which an authorised person can lawfully harm a seal. However, the Wildlife (Northern Ireland) Order 1985 does not contain any general defence for acts resulting in incidental harm to pinnipeds during fishing operations. Therefore, bycatch of pinnipeds may amount to an offence if the constituent elements of the offence are satisfied, no licence is obtained (and its conditions complied with), and no statutory defence is available.

Summary of the potential defences

In summary, the fragmented nature of these legal regimes produces differing levels of protection – and differing potential routes to defence – for marine mammal bycatch in UK waters. The defence under the Conservation of Offshore Habitats and Species Regulations 2017 reflects a nuanced approach that acknowledges the operational realities of fishing while requiring meaningful compliance with bycatch mitigation measures.

In contrast, under the Conservation of Habitats and Species Regulations 2017 (England and Wales), the Conservation (Habitats, &c.) Regulations 1994 (Scotland) and the Conservation (Natural Habitats, etc) Regulations (Northern Ireland) no such 'incidental result' defence is available.

In addition, under the Wildlife (Northern Ireland) Order 1985, which applies to pinnipeds (but not cetaceans), no incidental result defence exists.

Finally, under the WCA 1981, incidental defences remain available in limited circumstances.

SUMMARY

The UK's legal framework for addressing marine mammal bycatch is fragmented and legally inconsistent. Multiple instruments apply across different jurisdictions, including the Fisheries Act 2020, assimilated EU law, fishing vessel licence conditions and the various Habitats Regulations and national wildlife law. However, these instruments operate independently, with overlapping but uncoordinated obligations, and no single enforceable legal mechanism dedicated to reducing or eliminating marine mammal bycatch.

The Fisheries Act 2020 contains welcome objectives – such as to "*minimise and, where possible eliminate*" incidental catches of sensitive species – but these remain largely aspirational. No binding legal duty to avoid or reduce bycatch is currently in force, and fisheries licences require only the reporting of bycatch incidents, not their prevention or mitigation.

Crucially, although the various Habitats Regulations impose varying obligations to monitor the incidental capture and killing of Annex IV(a) species and to ensure that such capture does not have a significant negative impact, implementation is patchy. There is no statutory definition or defined threshold for what constitutes "significant negative impact", and no prescribed mechanism by which observed impacts must trigger legal or regulatory intervention.

The legal landscape becomes even more tricky when considering whether bycatch might constitute an offence under the various Habitats Regulations or national legislation, and whether there are statutory defences available. The Conservation of Offshore Marine Habitats and Species Regulations 2017 provide a statutory defence for incidental bycatch during sea fishing operations, provided mitigation steps have been taken and all other elements of the defence are met. However, no equivalent defence exists under the Conservation of Habitats and Species Regulations 2017, the Conservation (Natural Habitats, &c.) Regulations 1994 in Scotland or the Conservation (Natural Habitats, etc.)

Regulations (Northern Ireland) 1995. The result is legal inconsistency whereby fishers operating within UK territorial waters (up to 12nm from the baseline) may commit an offence for incidental bycatch, with no statutory defence available – even when acting lawfully and using best practice mitigation.

The overall result is a fragmented and inconsistent legal regime whose obligations are poorly understood, implemented and enforced, resulting in a failure to adequately understand the impact of bycatch on marine mammals in the UK and subsequently, failure to adequately prevent it.

CHAPTER EIGHT

CAPTIVITY, CAPTURE AND WELFARE

INTRODUCTION

The captivity of marine mammals – particularly cetaceans – has long been a subject of public scrutiny and regulatory concern, shaped by evolving ethical, scientific and welfare considerations. In the UK, the practice of keeping cetaceans in captivity has ceased – although it is not prohibited. This has been driven in part by changing societal attitudes and strengthened legal and regulatory frameworks. Pinnipeds, by contrast, continue to be held in various settings, including zoos, aquaria and rehabilitation centres, though their captivity is not without legal and welfare implications.

This chapter examines the legal framework that governs the captivity of marine mammals in the UK, focussing on the Zoo Licensing Act 1981 in England, Wales and Scotland,[1] and the Zoo Licensing Regulations (Northern Ireland) 2003.

The chapter also considers the implications of the strict protections afforded to marine mammals under the various Habitats Regulations and national legislation, particularly the offences relating to capture and the limited statutory defences available in cases of rescue, rehabilitation or humane euthanasia. These frameworks are especially pertinent in emergency response scenarios involving stranded or injured marine

[1] The Zoo Licensing Act 1981 Amendment (Scotland) Regulations 2003 (SSI 2003/174) amends provisions of the Zoo Licensing Act 1981 in Scotland.

mammals, where legal clarity is essential to ensure lawful and humane outcomes.

THE ZOO LICENSING ACT 1981

The captivity of marine mammals is governed by the Zoo Licensing Act 1981 (as amended), which establishes a regulatory framework for the inspection and licensing of zoos in England, Wales and Scotland. The purpose of the Zoo Licensing Act 1981 is to ensure that where animals are kept in enclosures, such enclosures provide a suitable environment – specifically, one that allows animals to express most normal behaviours.

Section 1 of the Zoo Licensing Act 1981 states that all zoos that are open to the public, with or without charge on seven or more days in a twelve-month period need a licence to operate from the local authority for the area within which the whole or the major part of the zoo is situated.

What is a "zoo" for the purposes of the Zoo Licensing Act 1981?

A "zoo" is defined in section 1(2) of the Zoo Licensing Act 1981 as "*an establishment where wild animals (as defined in section 21 [of the Zoo Licensing Act 1981]) are kept for exhibition to the public otherwise than for the purposes of a circus (as so defined) in England and otherwise than in a pet shop (as so defined)*".

Section 1(2B) of the Zoo Licensing Act 1981 makes clear that the Act also applies to zoos which are not open on seven or more days in a twelve-month period, but have a licence in force, such as those that are temporarily closed. The Zoo Licensing Act 1981 also applies to zoos that have closed permanently while they make arrangements for the future care or disposal of their animals.

The definition is broad enough to capture a variety of animal holdings, and whether a particular establishment falls under the Zoo Licensing Act 1981 is ultimately a matter for legal interpretation. To assist local authorities, the Department for Environment, Food and Rural Affairs (Defra) has issued guidance[2], which includes in its Annex B, a tool to help determine whether private animal collections or other establishments should be considered "zoos" under the Zoo Licensing Act 1981. However, the guidance notes that only the courts can make an authoritative determination:

> *"The Secretary of State is not in a position to give an authoritative statement on what is and what is not covered by the Act as interpretation of legislation is a matter for the Courts. However, the informal views [set out in Annex B of the guidance] may help local authorities decide whether collections fall within the scope of the Act."*

"Wild Animals"

Section 21 of the Zoo Licensing Act 1981 defines "*animals*" to include those of the class *Mammalia*, among others. It further defines "*wild animals*" as "*animals not normally domesticated in Great Britain*". The Zoo Licensing Act 1981 does not specify species or provide further detail on the interpretation of "*not normally domesticated*".

To assist with this, Annex A of the Defra guidance sets out Defra's informal view of what constitutes "*not normally domesticated*". However, the guidance again cautions that legal interpretation rests with the Courts:

> *"The Secretary of State is not in a position to give an authoritative statement on which animals fall into the "normally non-domestic" and "normally domestic" categories as interpretation of legislation is a matter for the Court. However, an informal view on the more common cases that have caused uncertainty is set out [in Annex A]*

2 https://assets.publishing.service.gov.uk/government/uploads/system/uploads/attachment_data/file/69595/zoo-licensing-act-guide.pdf

> *To explain the thinking, the two categories have been sub-divided into the following five sub-categories. Species not in categories 1 to 4 will almost certainly be in 5..."*

Sub-category 5 of Annex A includes *"True wild species, where domesticity is not seriously suggested. Examples: All species not listed in 1. to. 4."*

No cetacean or pinniped species are listed in sub-categories 1-4 of Annex A of the Defra guidance, and therefore, it can be interpreted that they are in sub-category 5, being "*true wild species where domesticity is not seriously suggested*".

On this basis, cetaceans and pinnipeds would be considered "wild animals" for the purpose of the Zoo Licensing Act 1981 and any establishment which is considered to be a "zoo" will require a licence to operate.

The Zoo Licensing Regulations (Northern Ireland) 2003

In Northern Ireland, zoo licensing is governed by The Zoo Licensing Regulations (Northern Ireland) 2003.[3] These Regulations require anyone operating a zoo to obtain a licence from DAERA. A zoo is defined in regulation 3(2) as:

> "*a permanent establishment where animals of wild species are kept for exhibition to the public ...*"

The Regulations do not apply to circuses or pet shops.[4]

Regulation 2(1) defines "*animals of wild species*" to mean "*animals not normally domesticated in the United Kingdom*". The Regulations do not

3 The Zoo Licensing Regulations (Northern Ireland) 2003 (SI 2003/115).

4 The Zoo Licensing Regulations (Northern Ireland) 2003, regulation 3(5).

specify species or provide further detail on the interpretation of "*not normally domesticated*".

It is suggested that the interpretation of "wild animals" set out in Annex A of the Defra guidance should apply also in Northern Ireland, especially given that the definition of "animals of wild species" in the Zoo Licensing Regulations (Northern Ireland) 2003 refers specifically to the *UK* (which includes Northern Ireland).

Regulatory implications

The designation of marine mammals as "wild animals" under the zoo licensing legislative regimes in the UK has important legal implications:

- Facilities housing cetaceans or pinnipeds for public display must comply with the licensing requirements and animal welfare standards under the respective provisions;
- These facilities are subject to inspection, including periodic visits by veterinary inspectors; and
- Local authorities are responsible for enforcing compliance and considering guidance when determining whether a facility qualifies as a zoo.

In practice, these legislative instruments set a high regulatory bar for any facility intending to keep cetaceans or pinnipeds. While historically, animals such as bottlenose dolphins were kept in public aquaria across the UK, since the 1990s, there have been no cetaceans held in captivity for exhibition. This reflects not only evolving public attitudes but also the significant welfare and licensing obligations placed on such facilities. There do, however, remain facilities housing captive pinnipeds – these include those for commercial purposes, as well as those undertaking rescue and rehabilitation for individual animals.

CAPTURE OF CETACEANS

As set out in Chapter 1, all species of cetacean are European protected species, being listed in Annex IV(a) of the Habitats Directive and are afforded strict protection under the various Habitats Regulations throughout the UK.

Offence of deliberate capture

Under the various Habitats Regulations, it is an offence to *deliberately capture* (and to recklessly capture in Scotland) a wild animal of a European protected species.[5] This prohibition is strict in scope and applies regardless of the animal's health or purpose of the capture. Accordingly, in the absence of a valid European protected species licence issued by the appropriate conservation body, any deliberate capture of a cetacean from the wild would be unlawful.

This offence is particularly relevant to discussions of captivity. Even if the intention is to provide care or rehabilitation (as opposed to display or permanent keeping), any form of capture or possession of a live wild cetacean could trigger this offence, unless a licence is obtained (and complied with) or a statutory defence applies and all of the conditions of the defence are met.

Statutory defences

There are limited and tightly framed defences to the offence of deliberate capture, which are designed to ensure that humane responses to injured or dying animals are not criminalised. These defences may arise where a

5 Conservation of Habitats and Species Regulations 2017, regulation 43(1)(a); The Conservation of Offshore Marine Habitats and Species Regulations 2017, regulation 45(1)(a); The Conservation (Natural Habitats, &c.) Regulations 1994, regulation 39(1)(a); The Conservation (Natural Habitats, etc.) Regulations (Northern Ireland) 1995, regulation 34(1)(a).

cetacean is found stranded, entangled or otherwise incapacitated, and human intervention is required.

Tending and release of a disabled animal

Under regulation 44(1) of the Conservation of Habitats and Species Regulations 2017, regulation 46(1) of the Conservation of Offshore Marine Habitats and Species Regulations 2017, regulation 40(2) of the Conservation (Natural Habitats, &c.) Regulations 1994, or regulation 35(2) of the Conservation (Natural Habitats, etc.) Regulations (Northern Ireland) 1995, the following defence applies to the offence of deliberate (or reckless in Scotland) capture of a cetacean where:

- The animal was disabled, and not as a result of the person's unlawful act; and
- The capture was done solely for one or both of the following purposes:
    - tending to the animal and releasing it when no longer disabled; or
    - releasing it after it had been tended.

This defence is particularly relevant to rescue and rehabilitation scenarios. For example, if a stranded dolphin is found on a beach and captured by a trained response team for medical care and subsequent release, the act of capture would not be unlawful, provided all parts of the defence are satisfied.

Importantly, the capture must not be for public display, research or other purposes – it must be solely for the animal's care and eventual release. The condition that the disability was not caused by a person's unlawful act also means that the defence is not available to those who have harmed the animal through illegal actions.

Euthanasia and disposal of a seriously disabled animal

Under regulation 44(2) of the Conservation of Habitats and Species Regulations 2017, regulation 46(2) of the Conservation of Offshore Marine Habitats and Species Regulations 2017, regulation 40(1) of the Conservation (Natural Habitats, &c.) Regulations 1994, and regulation 35(1) of the Conservation (Natural Habitats, etc.) Regulations (Northern Ireland) 1995, a person is not guilty of the offence if:

- The animal was seriously disabled, otherwise than by the Person's unlawful act, and there was no reasonable chance of its recovery; and

- The act was done solely for one or both of the following purposes:

    - ending the animal's life; or

    - disposing of it (other than by sale or exchange) as soon as practicable after death.

These provisions offer the legal basis for the humane euthanasia of stranded or mortally injured cetaceans, ensuring that emergency responders and veterinarians are not exposed to criminal liability where euthanasia is the only humane option.

CAPTURE OF PINNIPEDS

As discussed in Chapter 1, the principal legislation governing seals in England and Wales is the Conservation of Seals Act 1970 (as amended).[6] Under the Conservation of Seals Act, it is an offence to intentionally or

[6] The Conservation of Seals Act 1970 was repealed in Scotland by section 130 of the Marine (Scotland) Act 2010.

recklessly kill or take a seal.[7] There are exceptions to this offence, including the taking or attempted taking of any seal which had been disabled and was taken solely for the purpose of tending it and releasing it when no longer disabled[8] or where the reason for killing a seal which had been so seriously disabled and had no reasonable chance of recovering.[9]

In July 2025, the Marine Management Organisation (**MMO**)[10] advised that the relocation of 'healthy' grey and common seals that are not in need of medical intervention is classed as 'taking' of seals under the Conservation of Seals Act 1970, for example, where a healthy seal is in a dangerous location such as a road, urban area or near heavy machinery. The MMO's guidance defines a healthy seal as one that is mobile and alert and shows no visible signs of injury or illness, and is not a dependent pup (i.e., it has been weaned and is capable of independent survival).[11] Therefore, it is unlawful to carry out this activity without a licence. As of the date of the law in this book, licensing has only been implemented for England, though it is anticipated that the other jurisdictions will follow suit soon.

In Scotland, the Marine (Scotland) Act 2010 makes it an offence to intentionally or recklessly kill or take a live seal.[12] Under section 108 of the Marine (Scotland) Act 2010, the exceptions for alleviating suffering are set out as follows:

---

7 Conservation of Seals Act 1970, section 1.

8 Conservation of Seals Act 1970, section 9(1)(a).

9 Conservation of Seals Act 1970, section 9(2).

10 Section 9(1) of the Marine and Coastal Access Act 2009 transferred the Secretary of State's functions of granting and revoking licences under section 10 of the Conservation of Seals Act 1970 to the MMO.

11 https://marinedevelopments.blog.gov.uk/2025/07/09/why-you-need-a-wildlife-licence-to-move-a-healthy-seal/ (accessed on 31 July 2025)

12 Marine (Scotland) Act 2010, section 107.

"(1) It is not an offence under section 107 for a person to end a seal's life humanely (or to injure a seal when attempting to do so) if–

(a) it has been seriously disabled (otherwise than by the person's unlawful conduct),

(b) it has no reasonable chance of recovering, and

(c) ending its life –

(i) is the only satisfactory way to end its suffering, and

(ii) is not detrimental to the maintenance of the population of any species of seal at a favourable conservation status in their natural range (within the meaning of Article 1(e) of the Habitats Directive).

(2) It is not an offence under section 107 for a person to take a seal (or to kill or injure a seal when attempting to take it) if–

(a) it has been disabled (otherwise than by the person's unlawful conduct),

(b) it is (or is to be) taken only in order to –

(i) tend it with a view to releasing it after it has recovered, or

(ii) release it after it has been tended,

(c) it is (or is to be) taken only in order to –

(i) tend it with a view to releasing it after it has recovered, or

(ii) release it after it has been tended,

(c) it is (or is to be) taken in a manner and in circumstances unlikely to cause the seal to suffer unnecessarily, and

(d) taking it -

(i) is the only satisfactory way to help it to recover, and

(ii) is not detrimental to the maintenance of the population of any species of seal at a favourable conservation status in their natural range (within the meaning of Article 1(e) of the Habitats Directive).

(3) It is the duty of a person who kills, injures or takes a seal in a manner which is lawful by virtue of this section to report to the Scottish Ministers as soon as reasonably practical after doing so.

(4) Failure to comply with the reporting duty is an offence."

Practical application in the UK

In practice, these exceptions are most commonly relied upon by marine animal rescue organisations, wildlife veterinarians and response teams dealing with live strandings.

While the law recognises that emergency intervention may be necessary to assist disabled marine mammals, it sets clear limits on when capture is permitted without a licence. These provisions are not a loophole for captivity but rather a narrowly drawn safeguard to allow humane action in exceptional situations. Anyone acting beyond the scope of these exceptions – whether by retaining the animal for non-rehabilitative purposes or failing to meet the conditions – may face criminal liability.

SUMMARY

The UK's legal framework relating to the captivity of marine mammals is both restrictive and highly specific. The Zoo Licensing Act 1981 imposes stringent licensing, welfare and inspection requirements on facilities that hold cetaceans or pinnipeds for public exhibition, effectively creating a high regulatory threshold that no cetacean-holding establishments have been willing or able to meet since the 1990s. While pinnipeds are still held in captivity – primarily in zoos, aquaria and rehabilitation settings – the Zoo Licensing Act 1981's definition of "wild animals" ensures that their keeping remains subject to meaningful oversight and welfare protections.

Separately, the various Habitats Regulations, the Conservation of Seals Act 1970 and the Marine (Scotland) Act 2010 criminalise the deliberate capture or killing of marine mammals in the wild, save where tightly defined statutory defences apply. These defences are limited to exceptional scenarios such as tending to a disabled animal with the aim of release or humanely ending the suffering of an irreparably injured animal. Such provisions are not designed to facilitate or legitimise long-term captivity and must be interpreted narrowly. These frameworks prioritise the welfare of individual animals and the conservation of wild populations, while allowing a narrowly circumscribed space for human intervention in emergencies.

CHAPTER NINE

THE HOUSE OF COMMONS ENVIRONMENT, FOOD AND RURAL AFFAIRS COMMITTEE REPORT: A CALL FOR LEGISLATIVE REFORM

The fragmented and inconsistent nature of the legal protections afforded to marine mammals in the UK has attracted growing scrutiny from both scientific and legal communities. This concern was given significant political visibility when the House of Commons Environment, Food and Rural Affairs (**EFRA**) Committee published its report '*Protecting Marine Mammals in the UK and Abroad*' on 28 June 2023.[1]

The EFRA Committee found serious shortcomings in the UK's existing legal framework, highlighting its piecemeal and outdated nature. In a striking and unequivocal conclusion, the EFRA Committee stated:

> *"The legal framework to protect marine mammals is incoherent and not sufficient to effectively preserve these precious species. UK measures contain concerning loopholes and are in stark contrast to best practice exemplified internationally by the 1972 US Marine Mammal Protection Act.*[2] *In the short term, seals should be added to the list of*

1 House of Commons Environment, Food and Rural Affairs Committee, *Protecting Marine Mammals in the UK and Abroad*, Sixth Report of Session 2022-23, HC 697, Published on 28 June 2023 by authority of the House of Commons.

2 Discussion of the US Marine Mammal Protection Act 1972 and its merits is beyond the scope of this book.

> *species in Schedule 5 of the Wildlife and Countryside Act as soon as possible....*
>
> *In the long term, the Government should bring forward primary legislation on marine mammal protection."*

These recommendations reflect both the urgency of the threats facing marine mammals and the growing public and scientific consensus that stronger, clearer legal frameworks are needed. The EFRA Committee's emphasis on the need for primary legislation represents a significant and formal recognition that marine mammals merit a coherent statutory regime that consolidates the existing framework, fills legislative gaps and provides a platform for enforcement.

In response, the UK Government declined to commit to the development of new marine mammal legislation, instead pointing to ongoing work under existing frameworks. In its formal response, dated 24 October 2023, the Government stated:[3]

> *"We are still considering JNCC's extensive submission on the 7th Quinquennial Review (QQR 7) of Schedule 5 (protected wild animals) and Schedule 8 (protected wild plants) as required by Section 24(1) of the Wildlife and Countryside Act 1981 (WCA 1981). In the meantime, Defra have been working to raise awareness of the impact that disturbance can have on marine wildlife, including seals. Together with the Seal Alliance, Defra launched a Government-backed campaign in 2021, 'Give Seals Space'. As part of this campaign, Defra provided funding for signs to be put up on the banks of the Thames in early 2023 to further raise awareness of the impact of disturbance on seals and the importance of keeping dogs under close control.*

---

3 House of Commons Environment, Food and Rural Affairs Committee, *Marine Mammals: Government Response to the Committee's Sixth Report,* Sixth Special Report of Session, 2022-23, HC 1942, published on 31 October 2023 by authority of the House of Commons.

More recently, Defra published the Marine and coastal wildlife code for England in May this year. This provides advice and guidance to help people visit the coast responsibly and minimise disturbance to marine wildlife.

We do not expect to introduce bespoke primary legislation regarding marine mammals given the extent of legislation and international conventions which already exist."

While the Government's initiatives on public education and awareness-raising are welcome, its refusal to engage substantively with the EFRA Committee's call for primary legislation, or its recognition of the fragmented and incoherent status of current legislation is problematic for several reasons.

First, the Government's reliance on existing legal instruments overlooks the central concern raised by the EFRA Committee: that, as this book discusses, the current framework is fragmented, inconsistent and in many instances, incoherent. Such fragmentation makes the law difficult to understand, interpret and enforce.

Second, public awareness campaigns, while incredibly valuable, cannot substitute for clear and enforceable legal duties. Instruments such as voluntary codes of conduct or signage campaigns lack the legal weight necessary to prevent harm or ensure accountability. The suggestion that awareness-raising is a sufficient response downplays the scale and urgency of threats posed by activities such as disturbance, bycatch and noise pollution.

Third, the Government's claim that existing international obligations provide adequate protection fails to account for the limitations of those instruments in domestic law. While the UK is bound by various international agreements (for example, the Convention on Migratory

Species[4] and the Bern Convention[5]), these rely on domestic interpretation for legal effect. Where the domestic regime is fragmented or contains loopholes – as the EFRA Committee found – international obligations alone cannot ensure comprehensive protection.

Finally, the delay in deciding on amendments to Schedule 5 WCA 1981, despite clear recommendations from statutory nature conservation bodies and the EFRA Committee, signals an absence of political urgency. Chapter 1 discusses Schedule 5 of the WCA 1981 in more detail.

In summary, the Government's response falls short of addressing the legal challenges identified by the EFRA Committee. The current approach – relying on fragmented law and non-binding guidance – risks perpetuating uncertainty.

With respect to bycatch, the EFRA Committee report provided a critical assessment of the UK's current bycatch monitoring and mitigation efforts, highlighting serious gaps in implementation and enforcement. It concluded that:

> *"Current levels of bycatch monitoring are insufficient to gain an accurate picture of the numbers of marine mammals killed or injured in this way, despite the requirement for vessels to report marine mammal bycatch".*

While recognising the challenges faced by industry in adopting suggestions such as remote electronic monitoring, the EFRA Committee concluded that mandatory monitoring is non-negotiable:

> *"We therefore recommend that the Government introduces mandatory bycatch monitoring, but that this is phased over several years, with*

---

4 United Nations Convention on the Conservation of Migratory Species of Wild Animals.

5 Council of Europe Convention on the Conservation of European Wildlife and Natural Habitats.

smaller vessels being given extra time and, where necessary, financial support to meet their obligations. We would like to see an action plan to achieve this, with targets and milestones, by December 2023."

Beyond monitoring, the report underscored the urgent need for strategic, science-based intervention to reduce bycatch levels. It reiterated that bycatch is *"one of the grossest abuses of wild animal sensibility in the modern world"* and called for a step-change in the UK's approach to mitigation. While acknowledging that the Bycatch Mitigation Initiative[6] and Clean Catch[7] programmes have contributed positively, the EFRA Committee stressed that these efforts are not sufficient in isolation:

"We recommend that Defra and the devolved administrations work together to produce a UK-wide action plan with SMART targets to significantly bring down bycatch numbers. These targets should be developed in consultation with scientists, NGOs and the fishing industry and include consideration of risk factors such as location, gear type and species. Action should begin in the high-risk fleets cited by our witnesses as soon as practicable, and at the very latest be in place by June 2024."

The findings of the EFRA Committee Report are central to the analysis in Chapter 7 of this book. They reflect a growing recognition – at both political and policy levels – that the legal framework surrounding bycatch is fragmented, weakly enforced and insufficiently aligned with ecological priorities.

---

6 Defra policy paper, *Marine wildlife bycatch mitigation initiative,* published 10 August 2022. Available at: https://www.gov.uk/government/publications/marine-wildlife-bycatch-mitigation-initiative/marine-wildlife-bycatch-mitigation-initiative

7 https://www.cleancatchuk.com/

CHAPTER TEN

CONCLUSIONS AND REFLECTIONS

The legal framework governing marine mammals in the UK is vast and detailed – but it is also fragmented, inconsistent and complex. Over the course of this book, we have analysed the various statutory and regulatory tools that together aim to govern and protect marine mammals in UK waters: from the core offences under the national wildlife legislation and the various Habitats Regulations, to the designation and management of protected sites, the regulation of activities that cause disturbance, interactions with fisheries, strict conditions of capture and standards for captivity.

Taken in isolation, each of the instruments discussed provides a measure of protection to marine mammals. However, when considered together, it becomes clear that the system is not cohesive. Across species, jurisdictions and regulatory contexts, marine mammal law in the UK operates as a patchwork. This final chapter reflects on the implications of this reality and considers what a more coherent, future-facing legal regime might look like.

A fragmented framework: legal uncertainty and inequality

At the heart of this fragmentation is a misalignment between primary legislation and EU-derived regulations. While the WCA 1981 and the Wildlife (Northern Ireland) Order 1985 once formed the cornerstone of domestic wildlife protection, amendments in 2007 significantly curtailed their relevance for cetaceans, removing many species from Schedule 5 WCA 1981 and all cetaceans from the Wildlife (Northern Ireland) Order 1985, as well as narrowing the scope of applicable offences. In its place, the various Habitats Regulations have assumed increasing importance.

Yet, these are secondary instruments, which are now more at risk of future Government reform following Brexit and the assimilation of EU law.

This shift has had serious consequences for marine mammals. For cetaceans, protection now hinges on the continuation and interpretation of regulations increasingly vulnerable to reform and repeal. For pinnipeds, protections remain even more uneven – ironically giving greater protection to the rarely seen walrus than to resident species like harbour and grey seals.

The result is a system that is jurisdictionally uneven, difficult to navigate and inconsistent in its protections. This not only hinders enforcement but also leaves regulators, developers and stakeholders unsure of their legal duties.

Legal complexity in practice: protected areas, disturbance and captivity

Even in areas where progress has been made – such as the designation of SACs – significant challenges remain. SAC designation alone does not secure protection; it triggers a duty that must be followed through in project assessment, management and monitoring. Yet, the application of the HRA process to highly mobile marine mammals remains fraught with scientific and legal uncertainty. Baseline data are often incomplete, and thresholds for 'significant effect' or 'disturbance' are difficult to ascertain resulting in inconsistent interpretation.

The issue of disturbance encapsulates many of the challenges facing marine mammal law more broadly. Disturbance is not always direct or visible, yet it can erode individual health and long-term population viability. While guidance from the European Commission has clarified that disturbance includes impacts on behaviour, breeding and habitat use, the absence of binding thresholds or domestic definitions particular to marine mammals continues to create grey areas. In turn, this hampers both enforcement of offences and the implementation of licensing regimes designed to permit otherwise prohibited acts.

With respect to captivity, although there are currently no cetaceans held in captivity in the UK, and the combination of the high standards imposed by the Zoo Licensing Act 1981 and the Zoo Licensing Regulations (Northern Ireland) 2003, together with the strict provisions regarding capture of cetaceans under the various Habitats Regulations – there remains no legal prohibition in place. Keeping cetaceans in captivity remains possible under licence, subject to regulatory conditions. The absence of a complete legal prohibition continues to attract public scrutiny and concern.

Bycatch: a persistent and under-regulated threat

The incidental capture of marine mammals in fishing gear – bycatch – remains one of the most significant direct threats to their welfare and conservation status in UK waters. Despite longstanding recognition of the issue, the legal response remains limited and fragmented. Assimilated EU legislation such as the Technical Measures Regulation contains some aspirations and provisions aimed at reducing bycatch, but enforcement is inconsistent and data collection obligations are reported to be inadequately fulfilled. Domestic frameworks, including the Fisheries Act 2020, refer to sustainability as a guiding principle, yet contain no specific, binding duties to prevent or mitigate marine mammal bycatch. Meanwhile, the various Habitats Regulations theoretically prohibit the deliberate capture, injury or killing of cetaceans, but their application to bycatch is complex and has not been tested in practice. This legal ambiguity hampers effective oversight, frustrates efforts to achieve good environmental status under the Marine Strategy Regulations 2010, and leaves affected species – particularly harbour porpoise, common dolphins and pinnipeds – exposed to avoidable harm. Addressing this gap is essential to any future legal framework that aspires to be both ecologically credible and practically enforceable.

The EFRA Committee's call for reform: a turning point?

The 2023 EFRA Committee Report represents a significant moment in the conversation about marine mammal law in the UK. The EFRA Committee's unequivocal conclusion – that the legal framework is incoherent and insufficient – echoes many of the practical issues identified in this book. Its recommendations, including the immediate addition of seals to Schedule 5 WCA 1981 and the longer-term development of dedicated primary legislation, reflect a growing recognition that piecemeal reform may not be adequate.

The UK Government's response to the EFRA Committee's recommendations was notably cautious. While it pointed to awareness campaigns and non-binding guidance, it did not commit to new legislation, maintaining that existing measures and international obligations are sufficient. Whether or not one agrees with that assessment, it underscores the ongoing tension between legal adequacy on paper and legal effectiveness in practice. In addition, the recommendations made with respect to bycatch have both not been met.

Looking forward: principles for a reformed legal framework

As we look to the future of marine mammal law in the UK, several priorities emerge:

- Consolidation of existing laws: The current patchwork of offences, definitions and duties could benefit from integration into a single, more coherent legislative framework that does not regress on current standards. This would improve clarity, consistency and legal certainty.

- Harmonisation across jurisdictions: Legal protections should be consistent across the UK's nations. A more unified approach would ensure that highly mobile marine mammals are not subject to varying levels of protection based solely on jurisdictional boundaries.

- Incorporation of scientific evidence and local knowledge: Marine mammal law should be informed by the best available science and relevant and up-to-date knowledge.

- Robust enforcement mechanisms: Clear offences, enforceable standards and adequate resourcing are essential to ensure that legal protections are not merely symbolic.

- Future-proofing through principles-based law: The dynamic nature of marine ecosystems, technological development and advances in knowledge mean that legal frameworks must be adaptable. A principles-based approach could provide the flexibility needed to respond to new challenges without requiring constant statutory amendment.

Final thoughts

Marine mammals are among the most iconic and ecologically and culturally significant species in the UK. Their protection raises a number of legal, scientific and ethical questions, many of which have been discussed throughout this book. While the existing legal framework provides some important tools, it is not cohesive and it is not responsive to current and emerging risks.

The EFRA Committee's recent findings suggest there is appetite for improvement. Whether through legislative reform, regulatory clarification or more effective use of existing tools, there are a number of routes through which marine mammal law in the UK could be made more coherent and effective.

This book has sought to provide a practical and structured overview of that legal landscape – its foundations, its gaps and its potential future directions. As with many areas of environmental law, change may be incremental, but understanding the current framework is a necessary and vital step toward shaping what comes next.

MORE BOOKS BY LAW BRIEF PUBLISHING

'The Electronic Communications Code: A Practical Guide – Second Edition' by Kerry Bretherton KC, James Castle, Mark Loveday
'A Practical Guide to the Independent School Standards – September 2023 Edition' by Sarah McKimm
'A Practical Guide to Estate Administration and Crypto Assets' by Richard Marshall
'A Practical Guide to Parental Alienation in Private and Public Law Children Cases' by Sam King QC & Frankie Shama
'Contested Heritage – Removing Art from Land and Historic Buildings' by Richard Harwood QC, Catherine Dobson, David Sawtell
'The Limits of Separate Legal Personality: When Those Running a Company Can Be Held Personally Liable for Losses Caused to Third Parties Outside of the Company' by Dr Mike Wilkinson
'A Practical Guide to Transgender Law' by Robin Moira White & Nicola Newbegin
'A Practical Guide to 'Stranded Spouses' in Family Law' by Mani Singh Basi
'A Practical Guide to Residential Freehold Conveyancing' by Lorraine Richardson
'A Practical Guide to Pensions on Divorce for Lawyers' by Bryan Scant
'A Practical Guide to Challenging Sham Marriage Allegations in Immigration Law' by Priya Solanki
'A Practical Guide to Digital Communications Evidence in Criminal Law' by Sam Willis
'A Practical Guide to Legal Rights in Scotland' by Sarah-Jane Macdonald
'A Practical Guide to New Build Conveyancing' by Paul Sams & Rebecca East
'A Practical Guide to Inherited Wealth on Divorce' by Hayley Trim
'A Practical Guide to Practice Direction 12J and Domestic Abuse in Private Law Children Proceedings' by Rebecca Cross & Malvika Jaganmohan
'A Practical Guide to Confiscation and Restraint' by Narita Bahra QC, John Carl Townsend, David Winch
'A Practical Guide to the Law of Forests in Scotland' by Philip Buchan
'A Practical Guide to Health and Medical Cases in Immigration Law' by Rebecca Chapman & Miranda Butler
'A Practical Guide to Bad Character Evidence for Criminal Practitioners by Aparna Rao
'A Practical Guide to Extradition Law post-Brexit' by Myles Grandison et al
'A Practical Guide to Hoarding and Mental Health for Housing Lawyers' by Rachel Coyle

'Stephens on Contractual Indemnities' by Richard Stephens
'A Practical Guide to the EU Succession Regulation' by Richard Frimston
'A Practical Guide to Solicitor and Client Costs – Second Edition' by Robin Dunne
'Constructive Dismissal – Practice Pointers and Principles' by Benjimin Burgher
'A Practical Guide to Religion and Belief Discrimination Claims in the Workplace' by Kashif Ali
'A Practical Guide to the Law of Medical Treatment Decisions' by Ben Troke
'Fundamental Dishonesty and QOCS in Personal Injury Proceedings: Law and Practice' by Jake Rowley
'A Practical Guide to the Law in Relation to School Exclusions' by Charlotte Hadfield & Alice de Coverley
'A Practical Guide to Divorce for the Silver Separators' by Karin Walker
'The Right to be Forgotten – The Law and Practical Issues' by Melissa Stock
'A Practical Guide to Planning Law and Rights of Way in National Parks, the Broads and AONBs' by James Maurici QC, James Neill et al
'A Practical Guide to Election Law' by Tom Tabori
'A Practical Guide to the Law in Relation to Surrogacy' by Andrew Powell
'A Practical Guide to Claims Arising from Fatal Accidents – Second Edition' by James Patience
'A Practical Guide to Asbestos Claims' by Jonathan Owen & Gareth McAloon
'A Practical Guide to Stamp Duty Land Tax in England and Northern Ireland' by Suzanne O'Hara
'A Practical Guide to the Law of Farming Partnerships' by Philip Whitcomb
'A Practical Guide to the Law of Unlawful Eviction and Harassment – Second Edition' by Stephanie Lovegrove
'A Practical Guide to Costs in Personal Injury Claims – Second Edition' by Matthew Hoe
'A Practical Guide to the General Data Protection Regulation (GDPR) – Second Edition' by Keith Markham
'A Practical Guide to Working with Litigants in Person and McKenzie Friends in Family Cases' by Stuart Barlow
'Protecting Unregistered Brands: A Practical Guide to the Law of Passing Off' by Lorna Brazell
'A Practical Guide to Secondary Liability and Joint Enterprise Post-Jogee' by Joanne Cecil & James Mehigan

'A Practical Guide to the Pre-Action RTA Claims Protocol for Personal Injury Lawyers' by Antonia Ford

'A Practical Guide to Neighbour Disputes and the Law' by Alexander Walsh

'A Practical Guide to Coercive Control for Legal Practitioners and Victims' by Rachel Horman

'A Practical Guide to the Law of Driverless Cars – Second Edition'

by Alex Glassbrook, Emma Northey & Scarlett Milligan

'A Practical Guide to TOLATA Claims' by Greg Williams

'A Practical Guide to Elderly Law – Second Edition' by Justin Patten

'A Practical Guide to Responding to Housing Disrepair and Unfitness Claims' by Iain Wightwick

'A Practical Guide to the Law of Bullying and Harassment in the Workplace' by Philip Hyland

'How to Be a Freelance Solicitor: A Practical Guide to the SRA-Regulated Freelance Solicitor Model' by Paul Bennett

'A Practical Guide to Prison Injury Claims' by Malcolm Johnson

'A Practical Guide to Advising Clients at the Police Station' by Colin Stephen McKeown-Beaumont

'A Practical Guide to Antisocial Behaviour Injunctions – Second Edition' by Iain Wightwick

'Practical Mediation: A Guide for Mediators, Advocates, Advisers, Lawyers, and Students in Civil, Commercial, Business, Property, Workplace, and Employment Cases' by Jonathan Dingle with John Sephton

'The Mini-Pupillage Workbook' by David Boyle

'A Practical Guide to Crofting Law' by Brian Inkster

'A Practical Guide to the Law of Domain Names and Cybersquatting' by Andrew Clemson

'A Practical Guide to the Law of Gender Pay Gap Reporting' by Harini Iyengar

'NHS Whistleblowing and the Law' by Joseph England

'Employment Law and the Gig Economy' by Nigel Mackay & Annie Powell

'A Practical Guide to Noise Induced Hearing Loss (NIHL) Claims' by Andrew Mckie, Ian Skeate, Gareth McAloon

'An Introduction to Beauty Negligence Claims – A Practical Guide for the Personal Injury Practitioner' by Greg Almond

'Intercompany Agreements for Transfer Pricing Compliance' by Paul Sutton

'Zen and the Art of Mediation' by Martin Plowman

'A Practical Guide to Adoption for Family Lawyers' by Graham Pegg

'A Practical Guide to Industrial Disease Claims' by Andrew Mckie & Ian Skeate
'A Practical Guide to Conducting a Sheriff Court Proof' by Andrew Stevenson
'A Practical Guide to Vicarious Liability' by Mariel Irvine
'A Practical Guide to Applications for Landlord's Consent and Variation of Leases' by Mark Shelton
'A Practical Guide to Relief from Sanctions Post-Mitchell and Denton' by Peter Causton
'A Practical Guide to Equity Release for Advisors' by Paul Sams
'A Practical Guide to Financial Services Claims' by Chris Hegarty
'A Practical Guide to Financial Ombudsman Service Claims' by Adam Temple & Robert Scrivenor
'A Practical Guide to Running Housing Disrepair and Cavity Wall Claims – Second Edition' by Andrew Mckie & Ian Skeate
'A Practical Guide to Holiday Sickness Claims – Second Edition' by Andrew Mckie & Ian Skeate
'Arguments and Tactics for Personal Injury and Clinical Negligence Claims' by Dorian Williams
'A Practical Guide to Drone Law' by Rufus Ballaster, Andrew Firman, Eleanor Clot
'On Experts: CPR35 for Lawyers and Experts' by David Boyle
'An Introduction to Personal Injury Law' by David Boyle

These books and more are available to order online direct from the publisher at www.lawbriefpublishing.com, where you can also read free sample chapters. For any queries, call us on 0844 587 2383 or email us at mail@lawbriefpublishing.com.

Our books are all generally in stock at www.amazon.co.uk with free next day delivery for Prime members, and at good legal bookshops such as Wildy & Sons.

We are regularly launching new books in our series of practical day-to-day practitioners' guides. Visit our website and join our free newsletter to be kept informed and to receive special offers, free chapters, etc.

You can also follow us on Twitter at www.twitter.com/lawbriefpub.

www.ingramcontent.com/pod-product-compliance
Lightning Source LLC
LaVergne TN
LVHW052321200926
848481LV00002B/628
* 9 7 8 1 9 1 8 2 4 1 0 2 0 *